Walking CAPE TOWN

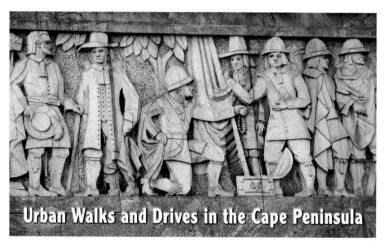

Urban Walks and Drives in the Cape Peninsula

John Muir

DEDICATION

This book is dedicated with love and gratitude to my wife, Linda, for her enthusiastic support over the years.

ACKNOWLEDGEMENTS

Thanks are due to Linda for the many patient hours she spent taking the photographs; our youngest son, James, for his amazing computer skills; and Joan Isaacs, Tim Ross-Thompson, David McLennan and Margot Morrison Muir for their expertise. I am also grateful to the many like-minded people involved in heritage conservation for their comments and information over the years.

My sincere thanks to the publishing team at Random House Struik for their guidance and professionalism.

First published in 2013 by Struik Travel & Heritage
(an imprint of Random House Struik (Pty) Ltd)
Company Reg. No. 1966/003153/07
Wembley Square, First Floor, Solan Road, Gardens, Cape Town 8001
PO Box 1144, Cape Town 8000, South Africa

www.randomstruik.co.za

Publisher: Pippa Parker
Managing editor: Roelien Theron
Editor: Mark Ronan
Project coordinator: Alana Bolligelo
Designer: Gillian Black
Cartographer: Liezel Bohdanowicz
Picture researcher: Colette Stott
Proofreader: Trish Myers Smith
Indexer: Michel Cozien

Reproduction by Hirt & Carter Cape (Pty) Ltd
Printing and binding: Toppan Leefung Packaging and Printing (Dongguan) Co., Ltd, China

ISBN 978 1 92057 294 5 (Print)
ISBN 978 1 92054 577 2 (ePub)
ISBN 978 1 92054 578 9 (PDF)

10 9 8 7 6 5 4 3 2 1

Front cover: Bo-Kaap (© Gillian Black). Insets: (top, left to right): Old port captain's office, V&A Waterfront; Houses of Parliament, Government Avenue; De Waterkant. Back cover: City Hall, Darling Street (© Gillian Black); map (Liezel Bohdanowicz).

Contents

Introduction	4
A Brief History	6

WALKS 10

Table Mountain	11
Company's Garden	14
Hiddingh Campus & Queen Victoria Street	20
Three Historic Squares	24
Adderley Street & St George's Mall	32
Long Street	40
East City	48
Bo-Kaap	57
De Waal Park & Gardens	62
V&A Waterfront	66
Fan Walk	76
Green Point	79
Sea Point	84
Camps Bay	88
Simon's Town	92
Fish Hoek: Jager's Walk	102
Kalk Bay	104
Muizenberg & St James	110
Muizenberg Village	117
Wynberg	120
Claremont	126
Liesbeek River Trail	130
Liesbeek River Walk	134
Mowbray	137
Pinelands	141

DRIVES 145

The Grand Drive	146
District Six	154
Woodstock	158
Rondebosch	162
Constantia & Tokai	166
Rondevlei Nature Reserve	174
Cape Flats	176
Blouberg & Durbanville	178
Tygerberg Nature Reserve	184
Best-kept Secrets	186
Bibliography	189
Index	190

Table Mountain forms a dramatic backdrop to the many attractions in the Company's Garden.

MAPS

Each walk and drive is accompanied by an easy-to-follow map. The Key to Maps, below, explains all the symbols that appear on the maps.

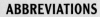

KEY TO MAPS

- Park, nature reserve
- Wine estate
- Parking area
- Building
- Pedestrianised street, square
- Point of interest
- **i** Information
- ⓣ Toll booth
- Ⓐ MyCiti bus service
- Rocky coast
- Railway line

ROUTE MARKS

- ⇄ Route
- ❶ Key number
- *START/FINISH* Walk start/finish

Introduction

This book is based on the places you will see and experience when you explore Cape Town on foot or during a road tour, and explains how they fit into the tapestry of Cape Town's history. It is important that we all attempt to conserve and retain the old buildings, and are able to continue to enjoy the scenic vistas and traditions of the Cape.

The chapters start with a series of urban walks and then proceed to places that need transport to access. In some cases, a combination of walking and driving will provide the best experience. Distance and degree of physical effort as well as facilities available along the route are included in each chapter. Street names and the names of buildings change with time and wherever possible street numbers have been supplied.

Detailed illustrated maps have been provided, showing the main landmarks discussed in the text as well as public transport facilities, where these exist. Start and finish points are clearly marked on each map.

I have included information about Table Mountain but have specifically avoided mountain walks and hikes, as there are some excellent books that cover this specialised subject.

All places mentioned that are open to the public are listed in the useful-information sections. Entrance to some places is free while others offer reductions for children and pensioners; where possible I have supplied these details. As opening times and admission charges change, I have given telephone numbers and website details where these are available. I also suggest you contact the nearest tourist information office for the latest information.

In suggesting areas where refreshments are available, note that it is not possible to provide a comprehensive list of all eateries and bars along each route. Instead, I have given a small selection of cafés, restaurants or pubs that might appeal to you. Where there is little or no choice along the route, I have suggested that you take your own refreshments. And remember to always take a bottle of water with you.

The weather in Cape Town is variable. It is not unusual for the city to have four seasons in one day, so make sure that you take a hat, sun cream, rain protection gear and warm clothing when you go out walking.

I hope you enjoy your time exploring the city as much as I have enjoyed compiling this guide.

Central Cape Town seen from
the top of Table Mountain

SHAEN ADEY/IOA

A Brief History

TIMELINE

1487
Bartholomew Dias sails around the Cape.

1503
Antonio da Saldanha names Table Mountain.

1652
Jan van Riebeeck arrives at the Cape on 6 April.

1657
Free burghers are granted land along the Liesbeek River.

1679
Simon van der Stel is appointed commander of the Cape.

1795–1803
The British take control of the Cape.

1798
The VOC goes bankrupt.

1803
The Treaty of Amiens is signed and the Cape is given back to the Batavian Republic.

1806
The Cape Colony comes under British control for a second time.

1814
The Anglo-Dutch Treaty is signed and the Cape becomes a colony of the British Empire.

1820
Settlers arrive from Britain.

1834
Slavery is abolished.

1840
A municipal system in Cape Town is instituted.

1854
The first Parliament of the Cape Colony is opened.

1860
The building of Table Bay Harbour starts.

1863
The first railway line between Cape Town and Wellington is established.

Although it is believed that the Phoenicians or possibly the Chinese were the earliest mariners to sail around the Cape, the first documented voyage was made by Bartholomew Dias, a Portuguese explorer who passed the tip of Africa in a gale in 1487 and named it the Cape of Storms. King John of Portugal realised this was the route to the East and renamed it the Cape of Good Hope. In 1497 Vasco da Gama left Lisbon to sail via the Cape to the Far East, returning two years later with a cargo of spices. In 1503 another Portuguese explorer, Antonio da Saldanha, named the large flat mountain rising above the bay Table Mountain, and he named the bay after himself – Saldanha Bay. Later, however, the Dutch took this name and gave it instead to the natural harbour further north on the West Coast, and renamed the anchorage Table Bay.

By the end of the sixteenth century, both the Dutch and the English were sending merchant ships to the East. The captains of some of these vessels would leave messages under rocks along the Cape coast, usually inscribed with the names of their ships and dates. Examples of these postal stones are on display at the Iziko South African Museum in Cape Town's famous Company's Garden.

In 1602 the Dutch East India Company (Verenigde Oost-Indische Compagnie – VOC) was founded in The Hague. On 6 April 1652, Jan Van Riebeeck, who had held several posts with the VOC, arrived in the Cape to set up a supply station to service the company's ships with fresh food and water for their voyages to and from the East.

The Cape was inhabited then by the indigenous Khoikhoi people, nomadic herders who moved about in search of grazing; occasionally, the San, who were hunter-gatherers, made incursions into the Cape Peninsula.

In 1657 'free burghers' were granted land along the Liesbeek River. They were former employees of the VOC who farmed to their own account, but were tied into contracts with the company. Slaves were brought from the East to work as labourers for the VOC and the burghers.

Simon van der Stel, the son of an official of the VOC, was appointed commander of the Cape in 1679. He established the eponymous town of Stellenbosch, prospected for copper in Namaqualand and settled the first group of Huguenots, religious refugees fleeing from persecution in Catholic France.

With time, the small settlement grew and a local economy developed. Towards the end of the eighteenth century, the trio of Louis Thibault, a French-trained architect, Anton Anreith, a German sculptor and woodcarver, and Herman Schutte, a German builder, started work on some of the Cape's most noted buildings, some of which survive today.

Although an outpost, the town at the southern tip of Africa was not immune to political changes in Europe and in 1795, after the Battle of Muizenberg, the British took control of the Cape until 1803. This was the era in which Lady Anne Barnard, wife of the British colonial secretary Andrew Barnard, produced her well-known journal and sketches describing life at the Cape of Good Hope. In 1803, under the Treaty of Amiens, the Cape was given to the Batavian Republic (as Holland became known after the demise of the Dutch Republic in 1795).

In 1806, after the Battle of Blaauwberg, in which the British seized control of the sea route around the Cape from the French, the Cape Colony came under British control for a second time. On both their military campaigns, the British attacked from the beaches on which they landed, steering clear of the fortifications surrounding the town. The strategy helped to minimise damage to the town's buildings. With the conclusion of the Anglo-Dutch Treaty in 1814, the Cape became a colony of the British Empire.

By the mid-1800s the town's administration was in a state of flux. In 1840 a municipal system was instituted and a board of commissioners and ward masters was established. At that time, the population of Cape Town was 20 000. In 1854 the Cape Colony received representative government and Cape Town became home to the colony's first Parliament.

Advances in shipping and a steady increase in the number of merchant vessels arriving in Table Bay eventually led to the building of a harbour in 1860. Three years later, the colony's first railway line – between Cape Town and Wellington – was constructed. The discovery of diamonds near the village of Hopetown in 1867 signalled the start of a period of prosperity for the Cape; it was soon to be followed by the gold rush on the Witwatersrand.

1899
The Anglo-Boer War breaks out. It ends in May 1902.

1910
The Union of South Africa is established on 31 May.

1948
The National Party wins the elections.

1950
The Group Areas Act is introduced, ushering in the apartheid era.

1983
The United Democratic Front is launched in Cape Town.

1990
Nelson Mandela is released from prison.

1994
The first national democratic election is held.

This statue in the grounds of the Houses of Parliament commemorates the golden jubilee of Queen Victoria in 1887.

·VICTORIA·R·I·
·1837–1901·

During the Anglo-Boer War of 1899–1902, Cape Town was the major British military headquarters for part of the conflict. The port was extremely busy with the arrival of men, horses, war materiel and supplies. The Treaty of Vereeniging, signed on 31 May 1902, brought the war to an end. Four colonies, the Cape, the Transvaal, the Orange Free State and Natal, were formed under British rule. Protracted negotiations followed, which eventually led to a national convention in 1908 and unification in 1910. The first Parliament of the Union of South Africa was constituted on 31 May 1910 with General Louis Botha as prime minister.

The early 1900s saw the city grow more rapidly and its civic management become more streamlined. By 1913, the greater municipality of Cape Town had absorbed most of the smaller suburban councils, with Wynberg abstaining until 1927, when the suburb was forced by ratepayers to join Cape Town because they wanted better services.

After World War II, the National Party won the 1948 elections with a majority of five seats. This marked the start of the apartheid era, followed in 1950 by the introduction of the Group Areas Act and, consequently, the forced removal of many thousands of people from their homes. Families were rehoused in hastily erected townships built with government subsidies on the sandy Cape Flats, a considerable distance

The pediment of the old Granary Building in Buitenkant Street was completed by sculptor Anton Anreith in 1814.

away from their former homes in District Six, Newlands, Mowbray and other suburbs that had been declared as being for whites only.

Ongoing opposition to the nationalist apartheid government culminated in the launch of a countrywide organisation, the United Democratic Front (UDF), in Mitchell's Plain on the Cape Flats in 1983, marking the start of the period known as the 'struggle years'. The UDF disbanded in 1991, more than a year after the release from prison of Nelson Mandela on 11 February 1990, when he addressed a huge crowd in Cape Town's Grand Parade from the balcony of the City Hall. Four years later, in 1994, South Africa's first national democratic elections were held.

Under the new democratic order, the municipal system was overhauled, with the city's various municipalities amalgamated into a single entity, the City of Cape Town, in 1996. Since then, the city has developed enormously. Precincts in the inner city as well as outlying areas have been redeveloped. The construction of Cape Town Stadium in 2010 – and the creation of an attractive urban park next door – has rejuvenated the Green Point area. In the city centre, the East City is destined to become a design and innovation district.

As the oldest city in southern Africa, Cape Town, the 'Mother City', combines over 350 years of modern history in a changing, dynamic environment.

The Houses of Parliament date from 1884.

SHAEN ADEYEMA

WALKS

Government Avenue
SHAEN ADEY/IOA

Table Mountain

Table Mountain

To visitors and Capetonians alike, the sight of Table Mountain is always inspiring, whether the view is from the deck of a ship in Table Bay, from a jet on its approach to the airport or from the crest of one of the mountain passes.

The iconic symbol of Cape Town is 1 086 metres high at its highest point, Maclear's Beacon. It is composed of sandstone, granite and Malmesbury shale. For those who live in the shadow of Table Mountain, it is an ever-changing kaleidoscope of beauty. It offers a different face on every side and can provide a visual 'barometer' of the weather for the day.

The mountain is part of the Table Mountain National Park, which stretches from the city to Cape Point, and is home to 1 400 plant species.

A cogwheel railway to reach the summit was mooted in 1907, and in 1913 a plan was proposed for a funicular to be built up Platteklip Gorge. In a municipal poll, ratepayers approved the scheme. World War I intervened, however, and it was not until 1925 that a Norwegian engineer, T. Stromsoe, presented the idea of a cableway. The Cape Town Aerial Cableway Company was formed and the cableway was opened in October 1929. Depending on the weather, the cable-car service operates daily and also on clear nights in the summer.

On the summit a number of designated paths lead the visitor to several viewing points. Look out for dassies (rock hyrax), a small mammal that is claimed to be related to the elephant.

USEFUL INFORMATION

Cape Mazaar Society
for information on kramats
021 699 0501
www.info@
capemazaarsociety.com

**Mountain Club
of South Africa**
for information on guides
021 465 3412

**Table Mountain
Aerial Cableway**
admission charge;
children under 4, free;
restaurant and gift-shop
facilities at the summit
021 424 8181
www.tablemountain.net

ADVICE FOR WALKING ON THE MOUNTAIN

- Always walk with someone who knows the route.
- Take a map and keep to paths.
- Take warm clothes and plenty of food and water.
- Carry a cellphone and a torch.
- Be off the mountain before dark.
- Watch out for mist and fog.
- Do not light fires on the mountain or pick plants.
- Tell someone where you are going.

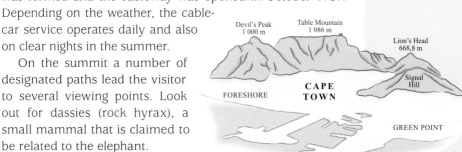
Devil's Peak 1 000 m · Table Mountain 1 086 m · Lion's Head 668,8 m · Signal Hill · FORESHORE · CAPE TOWN · GREEN POINT

The classic view of Table Mountain across Table Bay from Blouberg, with Lion's Head and Signal Hill to the right

There are five dams on the mountain – the Woodhead Dam (constructed in 1897) and the Hely Hutchinson (1904) are built across the Disa River at the back 'table', and the Victoria (1903), Alexandra (1903) and De Villiers dams (1907) are towards Constantia Nek. These reservoirs still serve the city but most of Cape Town's water now comes from dams further afield.

DEVIL'S PEAK

Named De Windberg by the Dutch, Devil's Peak is 1 000 metres high. When the prevailing south-east wind blows, it comes down Devil's Peak with great force. (The southeaster is also known as the Cape Doctor because the wind cools the city and was once thought to blow away prevalent airborne diseases.)

One of the Cape's legends concerns a Dutchman named Van Hunks, who continuously smoked a pipe filled with evil-smelling tobacco. The townsfolk objected to this habit and told him to go up the mountain to smoke his pipe. He agreed and used to sit on the saddle of Devil's Peak watching the ships in the bay while puffing away. One day he met a stranger wearing a hat who challenged him to a smoking contest. The competition lasted for hours until the stranger collapsed; when his hat fell off, Van Hunks saw the devil's horns. Meanwhile, a large cloud of smoke had formed over the mountain and this is the legend of the so-called tablecloth. The tablecloth of cloud cloaking the top of the mountain, a regular feature in summer, is a meteorological phenomenon caused by the condensation of moisture carried by the south-east wind.

LION'S HEAD & SIGNAL HILL

Lion's Head is 668,8 metres high and Signal Hill 350 metres.

When seen from De Waal Drive as you approach the city from the east, it becomes apparent why the Dutch called this landmark Leeuwenberg (Lion Mountain) – it resembles the outline of a lion lying on its belly.

The VOC placed a signalman on Lion's Head to warn of approaching ships by flag and cannon fire. In time, Signal Hill became the main signal post, with the local merchants relying on the flag signals to inform them of the arrival of ships in which they had an interest.

Signal Hill offers glorious views across Table Bay and the city. On the road to the viewing point is the kramat of Sheikh Mohamed Hassen Ghaibie Shah, a follower of Sheikh Yusuf of Macassar, who was exiled to the Cape in 1693.

Please observe the few basic rules listed on page 11 when walking or climbing on Table Mountain.

NOON GUN

The tradition of firing a gun in the city at noon began over 200 years ago, when it was used as a time signal for ships anchored in Table Bay. Originally the gun was fired from the small hill where the Royal Observatory is situated – in the suburb of Observatory. In 1902 the time guns were moved to the Lion Battery on Signal Hill and first fired there on 4 August 1902. The battery is manned by the South African Navy.

The two cannons, still in use, were cast in Britain by Walker & Company and bear the crest of King George III. The cannons were installed shortly after the first British occupation of the Cape in 1795, and were part of the old Imhoff Battery at the Castle of Good Hope. At midday in the city, they say you can easily distinguish Capetonians from visitors: locals glance at their watches when the noon gun fires, whereas visitors appear startled.

At the end of World War I, Cape Town began to observe a two-minute silence on the 11th hour of the 11th day of the 11th month (Armistice Day). The first minute was to remember the dead and the second to give thanks for those who survived. During World War II, the silence was observed daily.

Directions: From Buitengracht Street, take Upper Bloem Street. Turn left into the Buitengracht service road and then right into Military Road. The battery is at the top. Get there by about 11.30 a.m., as an explanation is given before the firing. It is open Monday to Friday.

Government Avenue

Company's Garden

Jan van Riebeeck's instructions from the Dutch company, the VOC, when he arrived at the Cape in 1652 were to find a place to build a fort and a garden to grow produce. The aim was to establish a refreshment station to stock the VOC's ships with fresh supplies. The streams from the mountain provided abundant water for passing ships and the garden.

Hendrik Boom, the master gardener, began work on the Company's Garden in 1652. The garden grew vegetables, fruit trees and medicinal herbs and plants. It was extended from its first site (where the Grand Parade is today) across Adderley Street and up towards the mountain. After a few years, it was about 18 hectares in size. It was surrounded by a hedge of ash trees and brambles. Incursions were made into

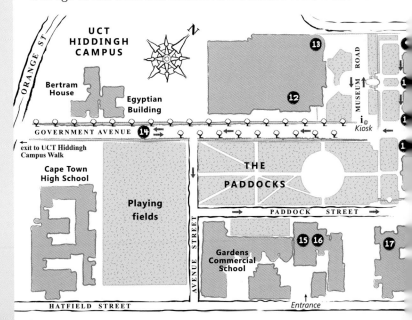

the area to provide a slave lodge and a hospital in the vicinity of present-day Wale Street. By the time Simon van der Stel became governor, sufficient produce was available from the free burghers and the company's farm in Newlands, so he converted it into a botanical and ornamental garden.

Today the garden is a green lung in the centre of the city, an oasis in a concrete jungle. It is enjoyed especially by the old, who sit on benches in the sunshine, and the young, who feed the pigeons and squirrels.

THE WALK

Start the walk at the entrance to Government Avenue at the southern end of Adderley Street, near the old Slave Lodge. Sadly, the grand entrance to the garden designed by Thibault was demolished in 1830. The Avenue was first planted with lemon and orange trees (the fruit helped prevent the sailors of the VOC from contracting scurvy). During Simon van der Stel's rule, these were replaced with oak trees, which are still there today. As you go along the Avenue, you will find the entrance to the Company's Garden on the right-hand side. There is an information board listing items of interest.

As you enter the garden, you will see the **Japanese lantern ❶**, which was presented to the city by the

Squirrels are a common sight in the Company's Garden.
GILLIAN BLACK

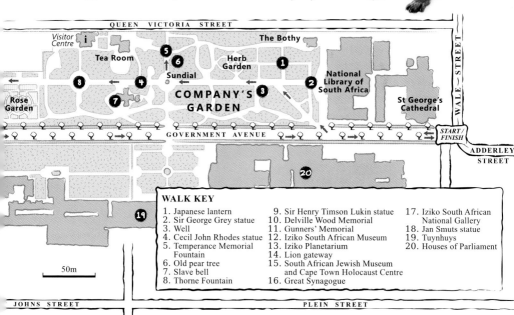

WALK KEY

1. Japanese lantern
2. Sir George Grey statue
3. Well
4. Cecil John Rhodes statue
5. Temperance Memorial Fountain
6. Old pear tree
7. Slave bell
8. Thorne Fountain
9. Sir Henry Timson Lukin statue
10. Delville Wood Memorial
11. Gunners' Memorial
12. Iziko South African Museum
13. Iziko Planetarium
14. Lion gateway
15. South African Jewish Museum and Cape Town Holocaust Centre
16. Great Synagogue
17. Iziko South African National Gallery
18. Jan Smuts statue
19. Tuynhuys
20. Houses of Parliament

Japanese Government in 1932 in recognition of the kindness and hospitality shown by Capetonians to a group of Japanese emigrants on the way to South America when their ship was delayed for repairs.

Nearby, facing the National Library of South Africa is a statue of **Sir George Grey** ❷, governor of the Cape from 1854 to 1861. Grey was a benefactor of the library and is portrayed with a book in his hand. He was also instrumental in securing funding from the British Government to build the first harbour in South Africa (see also Alfred Basin, page 66).

The statue of Cecil John Rhodes, with his hand pointing north, is near the tea room in the Company's Garden.

BRUCE BEYER/IOA

As you go up the main path towards the mountain, on the left is a **well** ❸ built in 1842 to provide water for the garden. Embedded in a tree is the pump handle, made in Milwaukee.

Straight ahead of you is a statue of **Cecil John Rhodes** ❹ by British sculptor Henry Pegram. Rhodes's hand points north and the inscription reads: 'Your hinterland is there.' (Rhodes believed that the future of Africa lay to the north and he had a plan for a railway to run from the Cape to Cairo.) Nearby is a sundial, which dates from 1781. It is thought to be of French origin.

On the right, just before you reach the Rhodes statue, is the **Temperance Memorial Fountain** ❺ of 1861. Made in England, this is a memorial to Howson Edward Rutherford, a member of the Cape Legislative Council. The memorial was moved from in front of the demolished Commercial Exchange Building in Adderley Street. Across the path, the **old pear tree** ❻ is said to have been planted in the time of Jan van Riebeeck and still bears fruit. The **slave bell** ❼, next to the aviary, is symbolic of the time when slaves worked in the garden and their daily toils were dictated by the bell. The support pillars were built in 1911/12. Dated 1855, the bell is reputed to come from the firehouse next to the Old Town House on Greenmarket Square (see page 28).

CECIL JOHN
RHODES
1855-1902
YOUR HINTERLAND
IS THERE

The **Thorne Fountain** ❽, a sculpture of a boy with a fish in a lily pond, was donated by William Thorne, the mayor of Cape Town in 1900. On the terrace above the rose garden is a trio of commemorations honouring the fallen in World War I. On the right is a statue of **Major General Sir Henry Timson Lukin** ❾, a South African military commander, sculpted in 1932 by Anton van Wouw. Lukin commanded the South African forces at Delville Wood on 15 July 1916 during the Battle of the Somme. The detachment had 121 officers and 3032 men. After five days' fighting, when relief finally arrived, just five officers and 750 men remained uninjured. As you head towards the Iziko South African National Gallery, you will encounter the **Delville Wood Memorial** ⑩. The memorial, a replica of the original, which was erected at the battlefield near Longueval in France, was designed by Sir Herbert Baker, a luminary of South African architecture. Further on is the **Gunners' Memorial** ⑪, which is dedicated to the 'Men of heavy artillery' who fought in World War I. In 1970 it was further dedicated to all artillerymen who laid down their lives for their country.

On the corner of Museum Road and Government Avenue is a small Iziko Museum information kiosk with a quirky metal squirrel on its roof. The **Iziko South African Museum** ⑫ stores and exhibits a vast collection of cultural, social and natural history artefacts. Next door is the **Iziko Planetarium** ⑬.

At the top of the Avenue, on the right, is the **lion gateway** ⑭, designed by Louis Thibault. It led to the lions' cages, which were part of a zoo established at this end of the garden by Willem Adriaan van der Stel, governor of the Cape from 1699 to 1707. The gateway on the left led to the antelope paddocks and the aviary. This gateway was reconstructed by sculptor Ivan Mitford-Barberton.

At this point, there is the option to exit

SIMON VAN DER STEL

Simon van der Stel was born on 14 October 1639; his birth was registered in Mauritius. It is claimed he was born at sea on the voyage from the East Indies. His father, Adriaan, was a prominent official in the VOC. His mother was Maria Lievens, whose grandmother was Monica of the Coromandel Coast, which means Simon van der Stel was of mixed descent. This is said to be the reason why he did not like paintings or sketches of himself. He returned to Jakarta and after both his parents died, sailed to Amsterdam at the age of 20.

In 1663 he married Johanna Jacoba Six, who bore him five children: a daughter, Catharina, and four sons, Willem Adriaan, Franz, Adriaan and Cornelis. In 1679 he was appointed commander at the Cape. His wife and daughter stayed in Holland, and his sister-in-law, Cornelia Six, accompanied him and his sons. He arrived in October 1679. He was promoted to the rank of governor in 1691. He retired in 1699 and died in Constantia in June 1712.

The Delville Wood Memorial commemorates South African soldiers who lost their lives during a World War I battle in France.

One of two statues of Jan Smuts in the Company's Garden, with the Iziko South African National Gallery in the background

and go to the Hiddingh Campus around the corner in Orange Street (see page 20), or to return along the Avenue.

On the return route, to your right, after the playing fields of Cape Town High School, is Avenue Street. If you turn into Paddock Street from here you can see the **South African Jewish Museum and the Cape Town Holocaust Centre** ⑮ (entrance in Hatfield Street). The museum recalls the contribution made by the Jewish community to South Africa's heritage and has a number of interesting exhibits. The centre, in the same complex as the museum, focuses on the chilling history of the 6 million Jews killed during Hitler's Nazi regime. The centre houses archival family histories about relatives of South African families affected by the Holocaust. Also in the same complex is the **Great Synagogue** ⑯, designed by Parker & Forsyth. It was built in 1904 and has a large copper-clad dome. Next door, the Old Synagogue was the first synagogue erected in South Africa, in 1862. The entrance to the Jewish Museum is through this building.

At the bottom of Paddock Street is the **Iziko South African National Gallery** ⑰, where you will find a mix of displays from its extensive art collection and contemporary special exhibits. The gallery is well worth a visit. Going towards the Avenue from the gallery, you will see the first of the garden's two statues of **Jan Smuts** ⑱. It was created by Sydney Harpley, a young British sculptor. Unveiled on 29 May 1964 to general public criticism, it received more newspaper coverage than any other statue in the Cape. Comments ranged from 'outrageous' to 'it looks like a baboon on a rock'. So strong was the outcry and concern that a public committee was set up to commission a new version (see page 24).

As you go down the Avenue, on the right is the **Tuynhuys** ⓭. This beautiful old building, with additions and alterations, was the residence of the Cape governors for over two centuries. It now houses the office of the state president. The medallion in the centre of the balcony depicts William of Orange; above him the infant gods Mercury and Neptune hold a drape with the VOC insignia. The building is not open to the public. A plaque commemorating the coronation of King George VI and Queen Elizabeth on 12 May 1937 is near the Houses of Parliament.

The **Houses of Parliament** ⓴ were completed in 1885 when the old Cape Parliament met there for the first time. It is possible to tour the building by appointment. Near the corner of the Avenue and Adderley Street, in the Parliament gardens, is a statue of Queen Victoria made in England by Thomas Brock. It was unveiled in 1887 in honour of her jubilee and was paid for by public subscription (see page 7).

Tuynhuys served as the home of a succession of Dutch governors. Today it houses the office of the Presidency.

DISTANCE
2 km

TERRAIN
Slight slope

EFFORT
Easy

USEFUL INFORMATION

**Centre
for the Book**
021 423 2669
www.nlsa.ac.za

**Iziko Bertram
House Museum**
admission charge;
children under 18, free
021 424 9381
www.iziko.org.za

**National Library
of South Africa**
021 424 6320
www.nlsa.ac.za

**St George's
Cathedral**
021 424 7360
www.stgeorgescathedral.com

REFRESHMENTS

- Cafés at Bertram House and St George's Cathedral
- Tea room in the Company's Garden

The old university Medical School, with its landmark tower, can be seen from Orange Street.

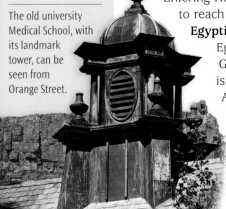

Egyptian Building

Hiddingh Campus & Queen Victoria Street

Hidding Campus in central Cape Town is the site of the country's first institution of higher learning, the South African College. Today it is part of the University of Cape Town (UCT) and houses the Michaelis School of Fine Art and the Little Theatre. This area was originally part of a menagerie, established by the Dutch at the top of Government Avenue.

This walk can be undertaken in conjunction with the Company's Garden walk (see page 15), or separately. If you combine the two walks, it is best to start at St George's Cathedral in Wale Street; otherwise your starting point is Hiddingh Campus on Orange Street.

THE WALK

Entering Hiddingh Campus, you turn left and then right to reach the old South African College, known as the **Egyptian Building ❶**. It was designed in the neo-Egyptian style by James Adamson and Colonel G.G. Lewis, and opened in 1841. The building is now used by the Michaelis School of Fine Art. Opposite is the **Little Theatre ❷**, built originally as a chemistry laboratory in 1881 and currently used by UCT's Department of Speech and Drama.

The **Hiddingh Hall ❸**, which nowadays contains a series of lecture rooms, was designed by the architectural firm Baker & Kendall in 1911. The building is named after its benefactor, Dr Willem Hiddingh. Adjacent to Hiddingh Hall is Bertram Place, dating from around 1880, and the **Iziko Bertram House Museum** ❹, completed in 1839. The museum building is the only surviving Georgian brick house in Cape Town. On the Orange Street side is the **old Medical School** ❺, built in 1911/12, and next to it is the **Michaelis School of Fine Art** ❻. Further down Orange

The Little Theatre (below) and the old Medical School (bottom) are part of Hiddingh Campus.

WALK KEY
1. Egyptian Building
2. Little Theatre
3. Hiddingh Hall
4. Iziko Bertram House Museum
5. Old medical school
6. Michaelis School of Fine Art
7. Ritchie Building
8. Rosedale
9. Centre for the Book
10. Bench (old Race Classification Appeal Board)
11. City and Civil Service Club
12. National Library of South Africa
13. St George's Cathedral
14. Von Dessin plaque

This embellished doorway led to the interior of the distinguished City and Civil Service Club, which occupied these premises in Queen Victoria Street until the turn of the twenty-first century.

Street, but still within the Hiddingh Campus, you will see the **Ritchie Building** ❼, originally built for the South African College School (SACS) by the architects Herbert Baker and Francis Massey between 1896 and 1898. This pair was also responsible for the design of **Rosedale** ❽, next door (1899–1902). As the gateways to Government Avenue have been closed off, you will have to return to the campus entrance, where you turn right into Orange Street. Walk towards the city and turn right into Grey's Pass, which becomes Queen Victoria Street.

The **Centre for the Book** ❾ was originally built for the University of the Cape of Good Hope. (This university was the forerunner of the University of South Africa, or UNISA.) It was later occupied by the Cape Archives until 1990. The imposing and impressive Edwardian building was designed by architecural firm Hawke & McKinlay, and built in 1906. The firm also designed the Supreme Court Building nearby.

Further down on the left is a bench with the sign 'whites/non-whites', which denotes where the **Race Classification Appeal Board** ❿ was located between 1959 and 1991, a reminder of the racial policies of the apartheid government. Further down on the left, at No. 18 Queen Victoria Street, is the building that used to be the **City and Civil Service Club** ⓫, designed by the firm Baker & Massey between 1896 and 1898. This former gentlemen's club used to have a distinguished membership.

Opposite, in the Company's Garden, is the **National Library of South Africa** ⓬, which was designed by William Kohler and opened by Prince Alfred, the son of Queen Victoria, in 1860. Sir George Grey was pivotal in raising funds for the building. He also donated to the library his personal collection of books.

On the right-hand side of Wale Street is **St George's Cathedral** ⓭, designed by Baker & Massey in 1901. It has beautiful stained-glass windows and an impressive interior. It is also known as the 'people's cathedral' because it welcomed people of all races during the apartheid era.

On the side of the Provincial Building, on the corner of Wale and Queen Victoria streets, is a blue plaque commemorating **J.N. von Dessin** ⓮, whose book collection constituted the foundation of the first public library in South Africa.

St George's Cathedral was designed by architects Herbert Baker and Francis Massey in 1901.

DISTANCE
3 km

TERRAIN
Slope up to Van
Riebeeck Square

EFFORT
Moderate

**USEFUL
INFORMATION**

**Central Methodist
Mission**
admission free
(donation appreciated);
open Monday to Friday
10 a.m. to 3 p.m.,
Saturday 10 a.m. to 12 p.m.
021 422 2744
www.cmm.org.za

**Church Street
Antiques Market**
Monday to Friday
9 a.m. to 3 p.m.,
Saturday 9 a.m. to 12 p.m.

**Greenmarket
Square craft stalls**
Daily 9.30 a.m. to 4 p.m.
in summer and
Monday to Saturday
10 a.m. to 4 p.m.
in winter

Greenmarket Square

Three Historic Squares

Three public areas played an important role in the history of Cape Town and in the lives of its citizens: Church Square, Greenmarket Square and Van Riebeeck Square.

Church Square served as a slave market before slavery was abolished in 1834. Greenmarket Square, as the name implies, was a fresh produce market in the eighteenth century. Van Riebeeck Square was originally known as 'Boerenplijn' – the farmers' square. While the architectural styles of the squares have changed over the years, each one has its own charm.

THE WALK

Start from the **statue of Jan Smuts** ❶ by local sculptor Ivan Mitford-Barberton at the top of Adderley Street. This was the second statue of Smuts to be sculpted and it was paid for by public donations as a result of objections to the first statue, which stands in front of the Iziko South African National Gallery (see page 18) in the Company's Garden.

The **Slave Lodge** ❷ was built by the VOC in 1679. It housed about 600 male and female slaves who worked for the company. Many alterations have been made to the attractive double-storey building

This statue of Jan Smuts at the top end of Adderley Street was sculpted by Ivan Mitford-Barberton.

The pediment of the Slave Lodge, Parliament Street, was designed by Anton Anreith.

we see today. After the second British occupation of the Cape, the Earl of Caledon instructed that the slaves be sold and the building was altered to house government departments. In 1810 the triangular pediment over the door facing Parliament Street was sculpted by Anton Anreith. It is

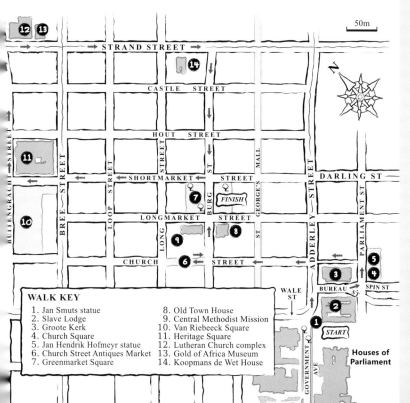

WALK KEY

1. Jan Smuts statue
2. Slave Lodge
3. Groote Kerk
4. Church Square
5. Jan Hendrik Hofmeyr statue
6. Church Street Antiques Market
7. Greenmarket Square
8. Old Town House
9. Central Methodist Mission
10. Van Riebeeck Square
11. Heritage Square
12. Lutheran Church complex
13. Gold of Africa Museum
14. Koopmans de Wet House

USEFUL INFORMATION

Gold of Africa Museum
(Martin Melck House)
admission charge;
open 9.30 a.m. to 5 p.m.
021 405 1540
www.goldofafrica.com

Groote Kerk
admission free
(donation appreciated);
open Monday to Friday
10 a.m. to 2 p.m.
021 422 0569
www.grootekerk.org.za

Iziko Slave Lodge Museum
admission charge;
visitors under 18, free;
open Monday to Saturday
10 a.m. to 5 p.m.
021 467 7229
www.iziko.org.za

Koopmans de Wet House
admission charge;
visitors under 18, free;
open Monday to Friday
10 a.m. to 5 p.m.
021 481 3935
www.iziko.org.za

Lutheran Church
admission free
(donation box);
open Monday to Friday
10 a.m. to 2 p.m.
021 421 5854

Old Town House
(Iziko Michaelis Collection)
admission charge;
visitors under 18, free;
open Monday to Saturday
10 a.m. to 5 p.m.
021 481 3933
www.iziko.org.za

REFRESHMENTS

■ Cafés and coffee bars in Greenmarket Square
■ Restaurants and bars in Heritage Square

SLAVERY

Jan van Riebeeck, the first VOC commander, required labour for the fresh agricultural produce he needed to supply to the company's ships. So in 1658 the first slave group of 170 men, women and children were brought from Angola.

Between 1658 and 1808, when slave trading was abolished in the British Empire, it is estimated that 63 000 slaves were imported to the Cape. For much of this period, there were more slaves than burghers. Most of the slaves were brought from India, Indonesia, Mozambique and Madagascar.

The Slavery Abolition Act was passed on 1 December 1834, and in 1838 the Cape's 38 427 slaves were set free. A comprehensive exhibition on slavery can be seen at the Slave Lodge in Adderley Street.

said that the sculptor was frustrated at being continually asked to include lions in his carvings, which perhaps explains why this particular lion looks a bit jaded. At the same time, changes to the building were made by the architect, Louis Thibault, and implemented by the builder, Herman Schutte. In 1926, the facade of the building was set back 13 metres when Adderley Street was widened. The alterations were done in keeping with Thibault's original design. The building now houses the Iziko Slave Lodge Museum.

Between Adderley and Spin streets is the **Groote Kerk** ❸. Its foundation stone was laid in 1700, making it the oldest Dutch Reformed Church in the Cape. The style of the building is a mixture of the Greek and Gothic traditions. The magnificent carved pulpit (1789) of Indian teak with heraldic lions is by Anton Anreith and carpenter Jan Jacob Graaf. The church was rebuilt to a design by Herman Schutte and dedicated in 1841. The most impressive feature is the vaulted ceiling with plaster rosettes, from which hang huge brass chandeliers. The clock tower and spire, which stand to the side of the main building, date from 1703. The statue outside is of Reverend Andrew Murray, who played a major part in the development of the Dutch Reformed Church in South Africa. Six Cape governors were laid to rest in this church. The headstone of one of them, Baron Pieter van Rheede van Oudtshoorn, is on the church wall on the clock-tower side.

Church Square ❹, across Parliament Street from the Groote Kerk, originally formed part of the garden established by Jan van Riebeeck to provide fresh produce for the VOC's ships. It was bounded by the Slave Lodge, the church and later by a spinning factory, which used slave children to weave silk from silk worms. The street between the factory building and the Slave Lodge became known as Spin Street.

On the traffic island in Spin Street is a plaque that reads: 'On this spot stood an old slave tree.' Slaves were auctioned here under a pine tree. Another memorial commemorating the history of slavery is to be found in Church Square, where the origins and names of slaves are engraved on granite plinths.

Also in Church Square, the statue of **Jan Hendrik Hofmeyr ❺** (1845–1909) was sculpted by Anton van Wouw. It used to be one of the few statues in the world showing a man wearing spectacles. Sadly, they have gone to the scrap merchants and will not be replaced. Hofmeyr is fondly remembered for his contribution to the Afrikaans-speaking community.

Granite memorials in Church Square engraved with the names of slaves commemorate the history of slavery.

Other buildings of interest on and around the square are No. 6 Spin Street – an attractive four-storey house attributed to Herbert Baker, circa 1902, and the imposing National Mutual Life Association of Australasia Ltd. The latter was built in two halves: the left-hand gable, dated 1905, was designed by the architectural collaborators Herbert Baker and Francis Massey, whereas the right-hand gable, which is dated 1933, was designed by architects John Perry and J.W. Delbridge. The building was restored for the Iziko Museums of Cape Town and houses the organisation's Social History Centre. At No. 9 Church Square, now the offices of Graaffs Trust, is a blue plaque indicating that it was the home of Dr John Philip between 1821 and 1846. Philip was the minister of the Union Chapel next door (No. 5 Church Square). The attractive Victorian building at No. 3 Church Square features ironwork thought to have been manufactured by Macfarlane & Co. of Glasgow, circa 1895.

From Church Square, go through the passageway next to the Groote Kerk, cross Adderley Street and walk up Church Street, past Newspaper House, and cross Burg Street. On weekdays you will find the **Church Street Antiques Market ❻** in a busy pedestrian mall, complete with coffee shops and buskers.

Retrace your steps to Burg Street, turn left and you will enter **Greenmarket Square ❼**. This was originally used as a vegetable market

This statue of the politician Jan Hendrik Hofmeyr (known as 'Onze Jan') is on Church Square.

by farmers, who brought their produce for sale to the people of the town. It was also used as a commercial centre where trained workmen, porters and horses and carts could be hired. Now the busy cobbled square is a market selling curios and crafts from all over Africa.

The bell of the Central Methodist Mission Church is known as the 'silent bell'; it has not been rung since the Golden Jubilee of Queen Victoria in 1887, when it rocked the foundations of the church.

On the right is the imposing **Old Town House** ❽, where the Burgher Council met after the completion of the building in 1761. The bell tower was later added to summon the citizens to hear important council announcements. In 1840 the town was granted a municipal council and the building housed the municipal offices and meeting chamber. In 1905 the council moved to the Victorian City Hall facing the Grand Parade. The interior of the Old Town House was then converted by architect J.M. Solomon into an art gallery. It houses the many works of art, including Dutch and Flemish masterpieces, donated by Sir Max and Lady Michaelis in 1914.

The circle on the doorstep of the Old Town House is the starting point from where distances to milestones along the Main Road to Simon's Town and later along Voortrekker Road to the north were measured.

On the corner of Longmarket and Burg streets is the **Central Methodist Mission** ❾, built between 1876 and 1879. Architect Charles Freeman and builder T.J.C. Inglesby were responsible for its Gothic style, complete with gargoyles on the exterior. The interior is also worth viewing.

Anyone interested in the art deco period will be delighted by some of the other buildings on Greenmarket Square. They date mainly from the 1920s and 1930s, and were inspired by the Paris Exposition of 1925. The Protea Assurance Building was built as the Sun Life of Canada Building in 1930. Its distinguishing feature was a golden, stained-glass window on the roofline, designed by the architectural partnership of Roberts & Small.

Regrettably, the window has since been painted white. The building was substantially renovated in 1965. Market House, on the corner of Shortmarket Street, was designed by architect W.H. Grant in 1932. In 2005 it was converted into apartments. No. 34 Shortmarket Street, Kimberley House, has ornamental balconettes among the vigorous art deco detailing. No. 40 Shortmarket Street was originally built as South West Africa House

Market House, built in 1932, is an excellent example of the art deco style.

in 1941; it is now known as Leadership House. Namaqua House, on the corner of Burg and Shortmarket streets, is another Roberts & Small design with prominent art deco touches. The Inn on the Square was originally designed for the oil company Shell by W.H. Grant. Known as Shell House, it was built in two stages: the Longmarket section was completed in 1929 and the central tower and remaining section in 1941. It is modelled on Shell Mex House, the company's head office in the Strand, London.

Continue up Shortmarket Street. Along the way, you will pass some old warehouses and town houses dating from around 1900. (We will pick up the buildings on the corner of Long Street on the Long Street walk, page 41.)

Across Bree Street (which was built wide enough to allow ox wagons to turn) is **Van Riebeeck Square** ❿. This was where farmers outspanned their oxen after long journeys from the country with provisions and cargo for the ships in Table Bay. The site was designated by the Council of Policy in 1772. The main building in the square is St Stephen's Church, built originally as a theatre by British governor Sir George Yonge in 1799. Yonge was determined that the colony's first theatre would open in 1800, so apparently he visited the site daily to check on its progress. It opened with a performance of Shakespeare's *Henry IV Part I*. Several workshops were built on the lower level to help finance the project. The church is not normally open to the public.

Heritage Square ⓫ is a group of old buildings bounded by Buitengracht, Shortmarket and Bree streets. It underwent a major redevelopment by the Cape Town Heritage Trust in the 1990s. A display board lists the history of the buildings in Shortmarket

St Stephen's Church was originally built as Cape Town's first theatre; in 1838 it was used as a school for freed slaves and a place of worship.

Street. No. 90 Bree Street was initially a two-storey Georgian town house, circa 1830, and is now the Cape Heritage Hotel. Original features include the stairs on either side of the high stoep (veranda) and what is claimed to be the oldest grapevine in the country, which you will find in the courtyard. Heritage Square has a number of popular eateries. No. 93 Bree Street is a typical example of a Cape Georgian town house. In the early nineteenth century, Bree Street stretched from the seashore to the then boundary of the town, Buitensingel Street. This broad street was a thoroughfare for merchants who built their homes with storage facilities next door, which were serviced by means of hoists. Yonge's theatre across the road on Van Riebeeck Square was the centre of social activity.

Walk up to Buitengracht Street, then turn right and cross busy Strand Street at the traffic lights. **The Lutheran Church complex** ⓬ is the oldest church complex in the country still standing in its original form. The Dutch East India Company followed a 'one faith' policy and recognised only the Dutch Reformed Church. But a growing number of German and Scandinavian immigrants started arriving in the country, and they adhered to the Lutheran faith. Martin Melck, a wealthy Lutheran, built what was described as a wine store and warehouse. It was said the building looked remarkably like a church. In 1776 the first unofficial Lutheran services were held in this building. In 1779 the Council of Seventeen, the policy-making body of the VOC, recognised the Lutheran Church on condition that the parson came from Holland. The following year, Reverend Andreas Kolver arrived and the storehouse quickly became a 'real' church. Today Anton Anreith's magnificent pulpit and choir stalls are much admired. The swan is an important symbol of the Lutheran religion and is shown both in the church and in the building next door, which served as the assistant minister's house. It now houses the Dutch Consulate.

Detail of the golden lion emblem outside the Gold of Africa Museum

Further along Strand Street, the **Gold of Africa Museum** ⓭ is in the old Martin Melck House, built in 1781. It is attributed to the partnership of Louis Thibault and Anton Anreith. Of particular interest is the *dagkamer*, a dormer room or garret above the house with a 360-degree view of Cape Town. Typical of a merchant's house, it would have allowed views of Signal Hill, the town and ships entering the bay. No. 94 Strand Street is an old warehouse once used by the Naval Commissariat. It blends in well with the Lutheran complex next door and forms part of the oldest city block in the country. Further down Strand Street are two attractive houses – No. 76 dates from 1810; No. 78 was built a little later and is now used as a café. Strand Street was previously known as Zeestraat, or Sea Street, named thus because the sea used to be close to this point before the present Foreshore area was built on reclaimed land.

The Lutheran Church in Strand Street was built by Martin Melck in 1771.

Koopmans de Wet House , a town house in Strand Street, dates from the 1750s. Louis Thibault restyled the facade of the house in the late 1700s. It was acquired by the De Wet family in 1809. A daughter, Marie de Wet, married Johan Koopman and after his death she and her unmarried sister lived in the house. Her house became an influential society salon and many well-known personalities visited Marie Koopman, including Paul Kruger, Cecil John Rhodes and Jan Hofmeyr. It is now the oldest house museum in South Africa. It is worth visiting for its interesting collection of furniture and ceramics.

Return along Burg Street, not because it is the most attractive route, but because it is the quickest way back to Greenmarket Square, where the walk ends. However, there are some interesting buildings along the way. No. 24, an ornate and decorative building, was previously New Zealand House. Opposite is No. 25, formerly Murray House, which must be the smallest 11-storey building in town. The Waldorf Arcade carries the name of the old Waldorf Restaurant, a favourite Cape Town venue that had its own resident orchestra. It flourished between the 1930s and 1960s, before being demolished in the late 1960s.

Flower sellers, Adderley Street

Adderley Street & St George's Mall

Adderley Street, the main thoroughfare in the city centre, is named after the British politician, Charles Bowyer Adderley, a proponent of colonial self-government. In 1849 the British Government wanted to establish a convict station in the Cape and proceeded to send a ship carrying a cargo of prisoners to the colony. However, the local population rallied against this initiative. Back in London, Adderley managed to lobby support against the proposal, and the ship, which was anchored in Simon's Town, was sent on to Australia. Parallel to Adderley Street is St George's Mall, a leafy and vibrant pedestrianised lane that links the Company's Garden with the Foreshore.

THE WALK

Start at the **statue of Jan Smuts** ❶ at the top end of Adderley Street and continue down the road to the Groote Kerk. A statue of **Reverend Andrew Murray** ❷ can be seen in front of the church. Murray, who was born in Graaff-Reinet in 1828, obtained a degree in theology from Aberdeen University and is remembered for his work in the development of the Dutch Reformed Church. From time to time, the statue's upraised finger gets damaged and it is rumoured that the church caretaker keeps a packet of plaster of Paris for repairs.

No. 25 Adderley Street was where **C.H. Pearne & Co.** ❸, once had its premises. Purveyors of 'Ladies Outfits, Mantles and Costumes', the shop was established in 1903. Its elegant facade masks a new development behind.

An early-twentieth-century shop facade on Adderley Street (below); the statue of Reverend Andrew Murray outside the Groote Kerk in Adderley Street (bottom)

ERHARDT THIEL/IOA

WALK KEY

1. Jan Smuts statue
2. Reverend Andrew Murray statue
3. C.H. Pearne & Co.
4. Old Barclays Bank Building (FNB)
5. Peace stone
6. Standard Bank Building
7. Old Stuttafords Building
8. Flower market
9. Wagenaar's dam
10. Blue plaque
11. War memorial
12. Station memorial
13. Jan van Riebeeck statue
14. Maria de la Quellerie statue
15. General Botha war memorial
16. Bartholomew Dias statue
17. Rotary tribute to Dias
18. Scott of the Antarctic monument
19. Old Colosseum Cinema
20. Atlas sculpture
21. Equity House
22. Argus Building
23. Old London and Lancashire House
24. Mandela Rhodes Building
25. Berlin Wall
26. Robert Gray memorial
27. Taj Hotel
28. Widow Twankey statue

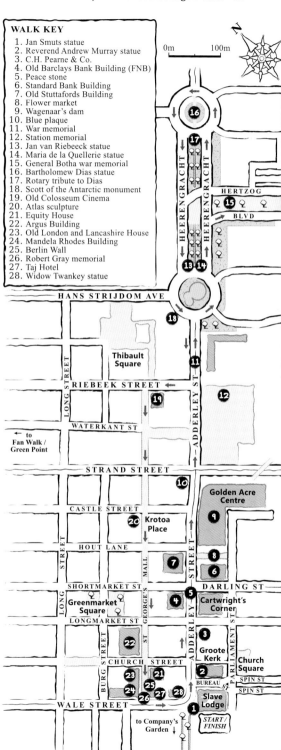

S·MON VAN DER STEL FOUNDATION

Sir Herbert Baker's last building in South Africa

Sir Herbert Baker se laaste gebou in Suid – Afrika

1933

STIGTING SIMON VAN DER STEL

The First National Bank was the last building Herbert Baker designed in South Africa.

The figure of Britannia on the dome of the Standard Bank Building

Across the road, the **First National Bank Building** ❹ (formerly Barclays Bank), on the corner of Shortmarket Street, was the last building Sir Herbert Baker designed in South Africa. It has a grand banking hall with a painted ceiling; when built in 1933 it must have been intended to rival the Standard Bank Building opposite. It is open to the public during banking hours.

Cross the road at the traffic lights and in the centre island is a **peace stone** ❺ with the inscription: 'Here Cape Town celebrated peace, 2nd August 1919.' Ahead of you is the **Standard Bank Building** ❻, which was designed in 1883 by architect Charles Freeman with two storeys. Two more floors were added in 1922. A statue of Britannia sits on top of the dome; the heads of Ceres, goddess of agriculture, and Poseidon, god of the sea and trade, are above the entrance.

Across the road, the building with the central flagstaffs used to be **Stuttafords department store** ❼. There were once four department stores on Adderley Street – the other three being Garlicks, Cleghorn & Harris, and Fletcher & Cartwrights.

The **flower market** ❽ in Trafalgar Place, off Adderley Street, is an old Cape Town institution. It is claimed that William Thorne, a mayor of Cape Town and part owner of Thorne & Stuttafords, arranged for the flower sellers to trade opposite his store in the early 1890s. Further down the block is the

Golden Acre Centre, built on the site of the old railway station. On the lower floor you can see the remains of the oldest dam in South Africa, built by **Zacharias Wagenaar** , governor of the Cape from 1662 to 1666. The reservoir was fed by the Fresh River and stored water for the VOC's ships. It measured 45 x 15 metres and was partly built of bricks brought from Holland. Across the road is a Simon van der Stel Foundation **blue plaque** ⑩ commemorating the site of the first private trading business in Cape Town, established in 1664. Diagonally opposite, a **war memorial** ⑪, sculpted by Vernon March in 1924, used to stand in front of the railway station, but was moved to the centre island further down Adderley Street. Inside the railway station, on the harbour side of the concourse, opposite the long-distance train platforms, is a restyled **memorial** ⑫ showing the history of the Sea Point railway line and the position of the old Monument Station.

At the circle around the fountain in Adderley Street, the road becomes Heerengracht ('gentlemen's walk'). There is a walkway along the central island that begins at the **statue of Jan van Riebeeck** ⑬, the first Dutch commander of the Cape. Sculpted by John Tweed, a pupil of Rodin, the statue was a gift of Cecil John Rhodes to the city in 1899. Next to this is a **statue of Maria de la Quellerie** ⑭. This statue of Van Riebeeck's wife was unveiled by Prince Bernhardt of the Netherlands in 1954 and was a gift from the Dutch Government. On the south side of the walkway, opposite Hertzog Boulevard, is a **war memorial** ⑮ to the ex-cadets of the South African training ship *General Botha* who died in World War II. In the centre circle, at the seaward end of Heerengracht is a bronze statue of the Portuguese explorer **Bartholomew Dias** ⑯, who sailed around the Cape in 1487. The statue was given to South Africa by the Portuguese Government in 1960. Returning along the walkway, you will come across another **tribute to Dias** ⑰; this one was funded by the Rotary clubs of Portugal and Cape Town.

This tribute to Bartholomew Dias on Heerengracht Street was funded by the Rotary clubs of Portugal and South Africa.

FORESHORE

A proposal to develop Table Bay Harbour by means of reclaiming land from the sea was first mooted by the South African Railways and Harbours in 1935. It included plans for the expansion of the rail service, with an extended area for passenger and goods purposes, as well as the enlargement of the central city area. The decision to go ahead with the plan was made in 1937.

The harbour expansion meant that Cape Town's pier had to be demolished. Opened in November 1913, at the cost of £85 000 pounds, the pier was 304,8 metres long and 13,7 metres wide. It provided entertainment facilities, swimming and boating at its lower levels. It was removed in 1938, to the regret of many of the city's citizens.

The harbour was designed to have a depth of 12,8 metres and a considerable amount of dredging was required. The spoil was used to reclaim the land between the dock and the shoreline. In all, 194 hectares were reclaimed, of which 67 hectares were used for the Foreshore development. The rest of the land was used for the harbour and the railway.

Although work on the harbour was completed in 1945, the development of the Foreshore continued throughout the 1950s and 1960s. In 1950 the Cape Town Foreshore Board was established, with three of its five members appointed by the government. The board was responsible for developing and administering the area, including naming the streets, drawing up design and planning rules and creating a list of building controls and regulations. It was disbanded in 1979, when the city council took over the administration of the area.

At the northern end of Heerengracht, at the intersection with Hans Strijdom Avenue, is a small monument to **Robert Falcon Scott** ⓲, the Antarctic explorer who, with four companions, perished in March 1912. His ship, the *Terra Nova*, called at Cape Town on the journey south in 1910.

Turn right off Adderley Street into Riebeek Street. The large art deco-style building on the corner of St George's Mall (named after the Anglican cathedral) is the old **Colosseum**

Krotoa Place commemorates a seventeenth-century Khoikhoi woman, Krotoa van Meerhof.

Cinema ⑲; it was designed by W.H. Grant and opened in 1938. Sixty years ago, this part of the city was theatre land. On the opposite corner was the Royal Theatre; up Riebeek Street was the Alhambra, an ornately decorated theatre that staged live plays and musicals; and one corner further up was the Van Riebeeck Cinema. Further along St George's Street was the Plaza, another art deco cinema, complete with milk bar next door. St George's Street, later renamed St George's Mall, was pedestrianised in phases during the 1980s and 1990s. Plaques along the mall mark these stages.

No. 52 St George's Mall was built for the Atlas Assurance Company in 1938. The **sculpture of Atlas** ⑳ supporting the globe is by Alan Howes; the architects were Hawke & McKinley. Krotoa Place, at the intersection of St George's Mall and Castle Street, commemorates a young Khoikhoi woman who acted as interpreter for Jan van Riebeeck. Krotoa van Meerhof, the first Khoikhoi woman to marry a Dutch settler, was born in 1642 and died in banishment on Robben Island in July 1674.

The sculpture of Atlas supporting the world was commissioned in 1938 for the Atlas Assurance Company.

On the corner of the mall and Church Street, at No. 107, is **Equity House** ㉑, which originally started as Norwich Union House in 1906. McGillivray & Grant were the architects. A sculpture of Justice is on the corner gable. The foundation stone was laid by one W.H. Hardblock!

At No. 122 is the **Argus Building** ㉒, known as Newspaper House, where the city's evening newspaper, the *Argus*, is produced. No. 148, a red-brick building that has been converted into apartments, was built in 1927 for the **London and Lancashire Insurance Company** ㉓. Together with other buldings on the block, it has become part of the Mandela Rhodes Place Hotel & Spa. The building on the corner of Wale Street, at No. 150 St George's Mall, is now named the **Mandela Rhodes Building** ㉔. Designed by Herbert Baker and Francis Massey, it was built in 1902 for De Beers Consolidated Mines Ltd. Outside the entrance in the mall is a concrete piece of the **Berlin Wall** ㉕.

SHAEN ADEY/IDA

The Mandela Rhodes Building, built in 1902 for De Beers, was designed by Herbert Baker and Francis Massey.

At the top of the mall is a **memorial to Robert Gray** ㉖, who was ordained as the first bishop of Cape Town in 1847. It was moved to its present location from the grounds of St George's Cathedral.

The two buildings on the corner of Wale and Adderley streets are now part of a redevelopment that houses the **Taj Hotel** ㉗. No. 119 St George's Mall was originally the South African Reserve Bank; its design won an Institute of Architects bronze medal for James Morris in 1932. No. 4 Wale Street, designed by architect G.M. Alexander and previously home to The Board of Executors, was built in 1894. Further floors were added later. A Simon van der Stel sign at the site reads: 'Site of the Hospital of the Netherlands East India Company, 1697–1782.' On the corner of the building is a statue of a shepherdess possibly guiding her flock. The piece has attracted ridicule among Cape Town's artistic community and has been nicknamed **Widow Twankey** ㉘ after the pantomime dame. One of the restaurants in the Taj has been named after the statue. The hotel has incorporated the graciousness of the two buildings in its redevelopment. This is a good place to stop for refreshments before returning to the starting point.

The statue of the shepherdess in a niche of the Taj Hotel has been nicknamed Widow Twankey.

DISTANCE
1,6 km

TERRAIN
Flat

EFFORT
Easy

USEFUL INFORMATION

Grand Daddy Hotel
021 424 7247
www.granddaddy.co.za

Long Street Baths
admission charge
021 400 3302

Pan African Market
open daily 9 a.m. to 5 p.m.
021 426 4478
www.panafrican.co.za

South African Slave Church Museum
admission free
(donation box);
open Monday to Friday
9 a.m. to 4 p.m.
021 423 6755

REFRESHMENTS

■ Long Street and adjacent streets are lined with bars, cafés and eateries serving Eastern, Western and Cape cuisines

■ At night Long Street is a popular entertainment area

SHAEN ADEY/IOA

Marimba band, Long Street

Long Street

Named Langestraat in 1790, and changed to its current name in 1809, Long Street measures about 800 metres from the old shoreline to the old city boundary of Buitensingel Street. In the mid-eighteenth century, this street had single-storey houses, which, as Cape Town and its residents prospered, became double-storeyed. The Victorian shopfronts and cast-iron work visible today were added later.

In the 1950s and 1960s, Long Street was divided into three distinct sections: between Dock Road and Strand Street were second-hand motor showrooms, bars and a nightclub; between Strand and Wale streets – a popular area for window shopping after work or at weekends – were furniture stores, four hotels and two furriers; and from Wale Street to the upper end of Long Street there were seven furniture stores (some second-hand),

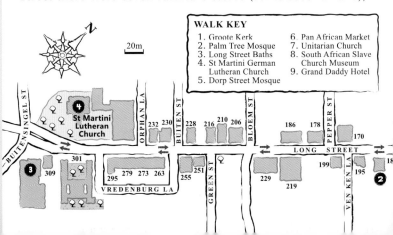

WALK KEY

1. Groote Kerk
2. Palm Tree Mosque
3. Long Street Baths
4. St Martini German Lutheran Church
5. Dorp Street Mosque
6. Pan African Market
7. Unitarian Church
8. South African Slave Church Museum
9. Grand Daddy Hotel

two bakeries, six butchers, four fisheries, three hotels and two hairdressers. This part catered mostly for the surrounding residents. A number of original shopfronts, doors and fittings have been preserved.

Today Long Street is a busy, vibrant street lined with restaurants, pubs and shops catering to tourists and locals alike.

THE WALK

Note that, as the names of businesses and shops are regularly subject to change, street numbers are given for easy identification.

Start at the corner of Strand and Long streets, and proceed along the left-hand side of Long Street towards Table Mountain to view the buildings with uneven numbers. No. 33 has the inscription on the parapet: 'H.C. Collison Ltd 1815.' This is probably the date the firm was founded. No. 35 is a typical Victorian building, circa 1890. No. 55 (D.M. Murray & Co. (Pty) Ltd) was for many years the home of Crawfords Carpets and Blinds; it was redesigned by architects Forsyth & Parker in 1934/5. No. 59, Langham House, was a former hotel, built in 1928; the fourth floor was added in 1941. No. 89, designed by Forsyth & Parker, was constructed in 1901/2 as the Imperial Hotel. The lion embellishment indicates that the establishment was owned by Ohlsson's Brewery. It then became the Green Hansom before changing to its current guise. Note the flying goose on the weather vane. The building numbered 107–111 was remodelled around 1890. No. 113 is Windsor House; the first two floors are probably older than they look – circa 1860. The third floor and pediment were added in 1922.

Antiquarian and second-hand bookshops add diversity to Long Street.

SHAEN ADEY/IOA

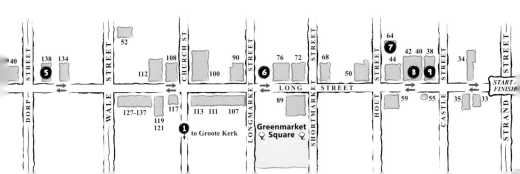

No. 175 Long Street is an attractive late-Victorian building dating from 1898.

At the intersection with Church Street, make a detour to see the Dutch Reformed Church – the **Groote Kerk** ❶ – in Adderley Street. Church Street, named in 1786, got its moniker from the fact that it leads to the Groote Kerk. No. 117 Long Street, built by E.K. Green & Co. as a bottle store, is described by John Rennie, a conservation architect who produced a comprehensive survey of old Cape Town buildings in the 1970s, as a 'late-Victorian showpiece'. Note the grapes and vine leaves in the plasterwork. Nos 119 and 121 are a pair of late-Victorian shops from circa 1900. Nos 127–137, on the corner of Wale Street, the former African Homes Trust Building, has an elephant's head carved by Ivan Mitford-Barberton out of pink Transvaal granite.

Cross over Wale Street and continue up Long Street. No. 175, designed by William Black, is an attractive Victorian building restored in 1986. On the corner of Leeuwen Street, the brick building was built as the Drommedaris Hotel.

No. 185 is known as the **Palm Tree Mosque** ❷ (or Dadelboom Mosque). This is the second-oldest mosque in Cape Town, after the Auwal Mosque in Dorp Street (see Bo-Kaap, page 58). It was built around 1780 as a single-storey structure; the upper floor was added around 1820. The building numbered 195–197 has a parapet dated 1895. The original wrought-iron balcony has been replaced with a concrete one.

The building housing Nos 199–205 has retained the original cast-iron and timber veranda. The central gable is dated 1896. The postbox on the pavement is monogrammed GRV, after George Rex V, the reigning British monarch at the time.

The building numbered 219–225 was constructed around 1895. It has a cast-iron veranda with so-called 'broekie lace' detail. The term, derived from the Afrikaans word for 'panties', was coined to describe the decorative embellishments found in cast-iron verandas and railings, suggesting they resemble the lacework of lingerie. Walter Macfarlane & Company of Glasgow mass-produced a great deal of these castings.

No. 229 has a long veranda; the building dates from about 1930. No. 251 Long Street, the former Mountain View Hotel and now home to a restaurant and bar lounge, dates from circa 1930. One of the only remaining trees in Long Street is located on this corner. The impressive four-storey building next door, known as Carnival Court, at Nos 255–261, was designed by English architect George Ransome. It was built as luxury apartments in 1902 with a two-storey veranda. Described as exemplifying Victorian fussiness, it has cast-iron columns and brackets made by Macfarlane of Glasgow. For many years, the much-loved Cranfords second-hand bookshop operated downstairs.

The Victorian building at Nos 263–271 was designed by John Parker and built in 1900. The removal of the balcony has made this building a little plain. The three-storey structure at Nos 273–277 was remodelled in 1940, with a number of different architectural styles having been incorporated in the redesign. Although the date of the gable is 1862, this probably relates to the earlier, single-storey building that originally stood here. Nos 279–283 is a simple two-storey building dating from 1900; the veranda has been removed. Built in 1930, No. 295 was an Ohlsson's Brewery-owned bottle store. It has a wavy Cape Revival-style parapet.

No. 301, Victoria Court, was built in 1930; it is an attractive apartment building with an enclosed courtyard garden. The building numbered 309–311 was built in 1897. It was originally

The iconic Palm Tree Mosque is the second-oldest mosque in Cape Town.

Lennons Pharmacy. A name plate in wrought-iron letters was once mounted on the roof ridge but has been removed. The architect was Anthony de Witt.

Next door are the **Long Street Baths** ❸, built in 1908; the architects were MacGillivray & Grant. The Turkish baths housed here were opened in 1927. Both facilities are still in operation and were revamped in 2005.

At this point, cross over to the other side to view the buildings with the even numbers on the way down the street.

The **St Martini German Lutheran Church** ❹ was designed and built by Peter Penketh between 1851 and 1854 in the early Gothic Revival style. The spire (which is a fibreglass replica of the original) is topped by a large cross. This is an impressive building, softened by the trees and space around it.

No. 232 was originally a house and was converted into shops in 1900 by architect John Parker. No. 230 was the Harp Hotel (circa 1920), another Ohlsson's Brewery hotel.

On the opposite corner of Buiten Street, the elegant, three-storey structure numbered 226–228 is dated 1902. No. 216, built in the Victorian style around 1900, has had another three floors added, but these are set back from the street. No. 210 was built as the Novel Flats in 1933 in the art deco style.

The magnificently restored Blue Lodge at No. 206 Long Street was built in 1900 as a boarding house.

No. 206, the Blue Lodge, is the most photographed building in Long Street. Designed by Max Rosenberg, it was built in 1900 as a rooming house. It is in the grand Victorian style with decorated attic windows, a turret and a weather vane. Note the wraparound wrought-iron balconies. The building fell into serious disrepair in the 1980s but was later restored.

The Victorian building numbered 186–196 contains a row of shops at street level and an attractive parapet. It still has its original cast-iron poles and balcony rails. The Cape Georgian door and fanlight is a central feature of Nos 170–176. Its parapet is dated 1897.

No. 148 was built in 1902 and known for many years as the Wiener Bakery.

The building was sensitively restored in 1982 and is a good example of how an old building can be rejuvenated.

No. 142, formerly Dorfman & Katz Furnishers, has a date on the parapet that probably refers to the establishment of the company. Note the art deco design in the upper section of the shopfront windows. No. 140, the Tyne Building, is from circa 1900. The balcony is a later addition.

No. 138 is the Noor el Hamedia Mosque, known as the **Dorp Street Mosque** ❺, built in 1884. The Daddy Long Legs Hotel (Nos 134–136) was once the home of Arthur Elliott, an American photographer who photographed scenes from the old Cape. A blue plaque recalls his presence there. The building is dated 1903.

When you reach Wale Street, turn left to reach the building at No. 52. Here you will see a sculpture of a horse's head protruding from the pediment. This building housed a livery stables in the 1890s before cars replaced horse-drawn traffic.

The Dorp Street Mosque was built in 1884.

Continue down Long Street. No. 112, the Twinell Building, with its Dutch-style gable, was designed by architect John Parker as a warehouse in 1920. No. 108 was another Ohlsson's Brewery hotel, the Johannesburg Hotel, built in the 1880s.

The building numbered 100–104, on the corner of Church Street, was constructed for Barclays Bank in 1935. It was designed by architect Gordon Leith in a grand classical style and features a solid granite stone base, pillars and urns.

The Pan African Market

No. 90 is a three-storey Edwardian building with a turret that imparts an Indian appearance. It was built around 1910.

The **Pan African Market** ❻, at Nos 76–80, has an interesting history. The original house was donated by Johannes Andries Bam to the Young Women's Christian Association after the death of his two teenage daughters from enteric fever soon after they arrived in Germany from Cape Town. Bam's house was demolished and the current building, designed by John Parker, was built in 1903. The commemorative panel reads: 'In memory of Minnie and Maria Bam. Founded 1886, re-built 1903.'

ERHARDT THIELJIOA

The facade of the South African Slave Church Museum is one of Long Street's many striking features.

Winchester House, Nos 72–74, is an attractive Edwardian-style building. The interior has been much altered but the pleasing exterior remains, along with the original tower. Architect William Booth redesigned No. 68 in 1900 and added Victorian embellishments, an extra floor and a tower to the two-storey building. The design includes a lot of fine detail.

No. 50 is where the old South African Permanent Building Society was located. Built in 1931, it has some attractive art deco touches on the upper floors.

Hout Street was named Oliphant Street in 1659. Its new name, conferred in 1790, is derived from the wood that used to be brought there from the slopes of Signal Hill. Pop around the corner to see the **Unitarian Church** ❼ at No. 64 Hout Street. Dated 1867, it has some notable Gothic touches. On the side of the old YMCA Building, on the corner of Long and Hout streets, is the foundation stone laid by Sir Alfred Milner in 1900.

The three-storey YMCA Building at Nos 44–48 Long Street was designed by Charles Freeman in 1883; the fourth floor was added later. A feature is the balcony on Long Street. At one stage of its life, the building housed the Space Theatre. No. 42 was the parsonage and later operated as a school attached to the former Sendinggestig (Slave) Church next door at No. 40, which is now the **South African Slave Church Museum** ❽. The church was founded in 1799 as a Mission Church. It is a landmark building, with striking exterior features. Inside it has Robben Island slate floors and an impressive pulpit, as well as balcony seating. In the early 1970s it faced demolition, but a major fund-raising effort, with the help of provincial and city council contributions, provided money to restore the building.

The Grand Daddy Hotel (top) has an Airstream Caravan park on its roof and screens movies during summer. The hotel elevator (above) is over 100 years old, making it one of the oldest in Cape Town.

No. 38, the **Grand Daddy Hotel** ❾, originally the Metropole Hotel, was designed by the Dutch architect Anthony de Witt in 1894 and underwent a rebuild in 1920. More recently, it has been modernised and features an Airstream Caravan park on the roof, and in summer shows outdoor movies. The lift must be one of the oldest in Cape Town. No. 34, a warehouse, was also designed by De Witt around 1904, despite the date 1896 on the building. The building is an attractive survivor of the turn-of-the-century vogue for terracotta facings.

DISTANCE
3 km

TERRAIN
Generally flat;
slight slope up
Buitenkant Street

EFFORT
Easy

USEFUL INFORMATION

Castle of Good Hope
admission charge
021 787 1249
www.castleofgoodhope.co.za

Central Library
021 467 1567

District Six Museum
admission charge
021 466 7200
www.districtsix.co.za

Iziko Rust en Vreugd Museum
admission charge;
visitors under 18, free
021 481 3800
www.iziko.org.za

REFRESHMENTS

■ Restaurant at the Castle and a variety of eateries and bars in the area
■ Look out for Charly's Bakery (Canterbury Street)
■ Eastern Food Bazaar is a food court in Wellington Fruit Growers' Building, Darling Street

The elephant carving on the Mutual Heights Building is by Ivan Mitford-Barberton.

Frieze, Mutual Heights Building

East City

For a long time this section of the central city has served as a semi-industrial centre. More recently it has been redeveloped as a hub for creative industries – from design to informatics – and many of the former merchants' warehouses now house flourishing new businesses. Historically, the area has some interesting buildings that are well worth visiting.

THE WALK

Start on the corner of Longmarket and Adderley streets. Longmarket Street runs from Buitenkant Street all the way to the slopes of Signal Hill, a distance of 1,8 kilometres, and passes Greenmarket Square – hence its name. On the corner of Parliament Street is **Mullers Optometrists** ❶, which sports an attractive art deco shopfront in black and chrome.

Across the road is the **Old Mutual Building** ❷ (now an apartment building known as Mutual Heights), with its magnificent continuous frieze of carved stone depicting different

facets of South Africa's history. The frieze, which runs along the three visible sides of the building, was created by sculptor Ivan Mitford-Barberton. The enormous granite animal cornerstones are especially noteworthy. The building, with art deco features, was designed by the architectural firm Louw & Louw, in association with F.M. Glennie.

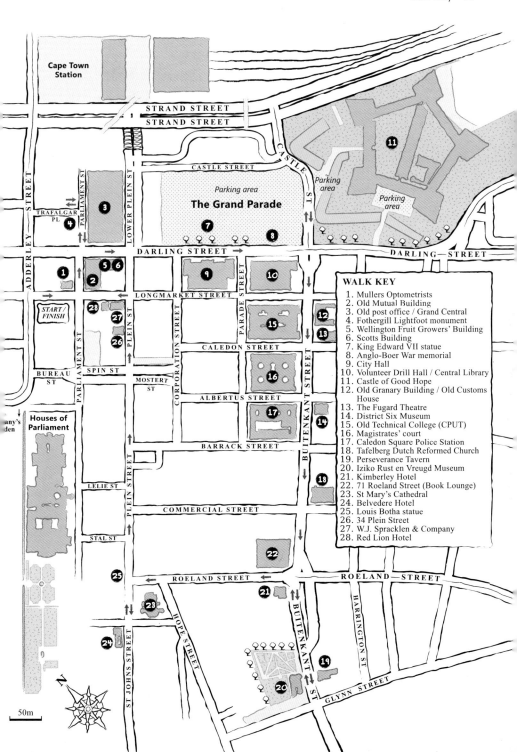

Cape Town Station

STRAND STREET
STRAND STREET

CASTLE STREET

Parking area
The Grand Parade

Parking area

Parking area

DARLING STREET
DARLING STREET

TRAFALGAR PL

LONGMARKET STREET

CALEDON STREET

ALBERTUS STREET

BARRACK STREET

COMMERCIAL STREET

ROELAND STREET
ROELAND STREET

ADDERLEY STREET
PARLIAMENT ST
LOWER PLEIN ST
CASTLE ST
PARADE STREET
CORPORATION STREET
BUITENKANT STREET
PLEIN ST

BUREAU ST
SPIN ST
MOSTERT ST
PARLIAMENT ST
LELIE ST
STAL ST
PLEIN STREET
ST JOHNS STREET
HOPE STREET
BUITENKANT ST
HARRINGTON ST
GLYNN STREET

START / FINISH

Houses of Parliament

any's den

WALK KEY

1. Mullers Optometrists
2. Old Mutual Building
3. Old post office / Grand Central
4. Fothergill Lightfoot monument
5. Wellington Fruit Growers' Building
6. Scotts Building
7. King Edward VII statue
8. Anglo-Boer War memorial
9. City Hall
10. Volunteer Drill Hall / Central Library
11. Castle of Good Hope
12. Old Granary Building / Old Customs House
13. The Fugard Theatre
14. District Six Museum
15. Old Technical College (CPUT)
16. Magistrates' court
17. Caledon Square Police Station
18. Tafelberg Dutch Reformed Church
19. Perseverance Tavern
20. Iziko Rust en Vreugd Museum
21. Kimberley Hotel
22. 71 Roeland Street (Book Lounge)
23. St Mary's Cathedral
24. Belvedere Hotel
25. Louis Botha statue
26. 34 Plein Street
27. W.J. Spracklen & Company
28. Red Lion Hotel

N

50m

Opposite, the **old post office** has been renamed **Grand Central ❸**. The post office had a large banking hall with a central counter that remains, and has been changed into a market. The main features of the hall are the six large murals. The first two are by J.M. Amshewitz and depict Jan van Riebeeck and Lady Anne Barnard arriving at the Castle. Another pair, painted by G.W. Pilkington, shows the *Union-Castle* mail boat and the arrival of the 1820 settlers. The murals of the Cape Dutch homestead and the Malay Quarter are the works of Sydney Carter. The building opened in 1940.

Across Parliament Street, in front of the Trafalgar Place flower market is a monument to **Thomas Fothergill Lightfoot ❹**, archdeacon of the Anglican Church. He was known as the Southeaster, as he was as swift and vigorous as the wind in looking after his parishioners. He translated part of the English Prayerbook into High Dutch and started an adult school for mechanics. During the smallpox epidemic, he regularly visited the Somerset Hospital, where a ward in the old section is named after him. Ironically, he died partly as a result of injuries he sustained when he was blown over by a strong gust of Cape Town's infamous south-east wind. And three years after it was erected, the monument was also blown over by the wind!

Back in Darling Street (named after acting governor Charles Darling in 1854), next to the Old Mutual Building is the **Wellington Fruit Growers' Building ❺**, dated 1902. It is attractively designed in salmon terracotta by architects Baker & Massey.

Scotts Building ❻, on the corner of Darling and Plein streets, was designed by W.H. Grant circa 1933 and has distinctive art deco features. This was the site of the popular Tivoli Theatre music hall.

Continue along Darling Street to the Grand Parade. This was originally double its present size and used for military exercises. A section of the boundary wall can be seen opposite the Castle of Good Hope. The Grand Parade was remodelled in 2006 and

Murals such as these of Lady Anne Barnard (top) and the Union-Castle mail ship (above) can be seen in the old banking hall in the Grand Central Building.

has lost some of its character. There are two memorials here. On the axis of the City Hall is a statue of **King Edward VII** ❼, Queen Victoria's eldest son. Created by William Goscombe John (R.A.), the statue was completed in 1904. The striking **Anglo-Boer War memorial** ❽ is also by Goscombe John. Its inscription reads: 'To the undying honour of those sons of the city who gave their lives for the love of the Motherland and in defence of the Colony during the Anglo-Boer War 1899–1902. This memorial is erected by the citizens of Cape Town ... Never king had more loyal subjects.' The roll of honour includes names from the Cape Garrison Artillery, The Duke of Edinburgh's own Volunteer Rifles and B Company, Cape Medical Corps.

Built in the Italian Renaissance style, the **City Hall** ❾ was inaugurated on 25 July 1905. In 1894 a competition was held for the design of the building, and out of the 17 entrants, the firm of Reid & Green was selected as the winner. The cornerstone is dated 1900. The main entrance in Darling Street

Cape Town's City Hall was opened in 1905.

has a handsome balustrade and carved stone portico, with the balcony supported by columns of red Aberdeen granite. From this balcony, former President Nelson Mandela addressed the crowds in 1990 on his release from prison. The clock is half the size of Big Ben; the clock tower also houses the carillon, whose bells are dedicated to those who died in World War I.

Next door is the **Volunteer Drill Hall** ❿. This was built for the volunteer military regiments and opened on 15 December 1885. Some military motifs are visible on the exterior walls. The building has been converted into an excellent three-floor public library, the Central Library.

Construction of the **Castle of Good Hope** ⓫ nearby began in 1666. It was completed in 1679,

SHAEN J.DEY/IOA

The Castle of Good Hope's historic entrance gate (top) and cannon (above)

and the wooden fort Van Riebeeck had built on the side of the parade next to today's Golden Acre mall was then demolished. The Castle is built in the shape of a pentagon with a bastion at each corner. These are named after the titles of the Prince of Orange. The northern bastion is Buren; the eastern point is Katzenellenbogen; in the south-east corner is Nassau; Orange is the south-west bastion; and the western point is Leerdam.

The original entrance to the Castle faced the sea; the entrance used today was built in 1684. The original bell, cast in Holland and installed in 1697, still hangs in the bell tower above the entrance. Carved on the architrave, below the pediment, are the coats of arms of the Dutch towns where the Dutch East India Company had chambers. Through the gates is the centrepiece of the Castle: the magnificent *De Kat* balcony.

Today, while still partially used for military purposes, the Castle is a popular tourist attraction, offering guided tours, horse-drawn carriage rides and displays that include paintings, maps and sketches from the William Fehr Collection.

Coming out of the Castle, turn left and go up Buitenkant Street. Until the end of the eighteenth century, this was the southern boundary of the town.

On the corner with Longmarket Street is the superb **old Granary Building 12**, also known as the Old Customs House. The facade, the work of Anton Anreith, has the figures of Neptune and Britannia, as well as a coat of arms displaying a lion and unicorn, and the date, 1814.

Gateway and pediment of the Castle of Good Hope

ALL WHO PASS

REMEMBER THE THOUSANDS OF PEOPLE WHO LIVED
FOR GENERATIONS IN DISTRICT SIX
AND WERE FORCED BY LAW TO LEAVE THEIR HOMES
BECAUSE OF THE COLOUR OF THEIR SKINS.
REMEMBER ST. MARKS CHURCH AND THE COMMUNITY
WHO RESISTED THE DESTRUCTION OF DISTRICT SIX

Hands Off District Six Campaign 11.2.1989

A plaque erected
by the Methodist
Church outside
the District Six
Museum

The Fugard Theatre ⑬ is in the old Sacks Futeran centre, on the corner of Buitenkant and Caledon streets.

The building currently housing the **District Six Museum** ⑭ was originally a wine store. It was converted into the Methodist Central Mission Church in 1882, and an attractive cast-iron gallery was added in 1902. The museum's many displays cover the history of District Six, an old residential part of the city, from where thousands of people were forcibly removed to mainly the Cape Flats (see page 176) in the 1960s and 1970s when District Six was designated a whites-only area by the apartheid government. One of the museum's exhibitions is a display of the old street name boards used in District Six. A plaque at the door erected by the Methodist Church reads: 'All who pass remember the thousands of people who lived for generations in District Six and were forced by law to leave their homes because of the colour of their skins.'

Further along, on the right-hand side of Buitenkant Street, is the old **Cape Technical College** ⑮, built from 1921 to 1923. It is now known as the Cape Peninsula University of Technology.

The District Six
Museum

SHAEN ADEY/IOA

PASS-LAW PROTESTS: THE 1960 MARCH

In 1952 the newly elected National Party passed legislation to control the movement of Africans by making it compulsory for all black South Africans over the age of 16 to carry a 'pass book', especially when in designated white areas. In response to the proclamation of the Abolition of Passes and Co-ordination of Documents Act, the ANC launched the Defiance Campaign in 1952.

Some years later, in early 1960, a breakaway group from the ANC, the Pan Africanist Congress (PAC), led by Robert Sobukwe, announced the launch of its own anti-pass campaign. The protest, which got off to a start on 22 March, found appeal in parts of the country. In Cape Town several protests resulted in deaths and injuries following police action in the townships. A work stayaway was initiated, which led to police entering houses in Langa and Nyanga to force people to go to work.

On 31 March 1960, the PAC's regional secretary in the Cape, 23-year-old Philip Kgosana, led a march of approximately 30 000 people to Parliament. After speaking to a friend in Parliament, Eulalie Stott, a Black Sash member and Newlands housewife, established that Parliament was being protected by the army with machine guns. Determined to warn Kgosana, she drove her car to De Waal Drive, past the marchers, to deliver the message. On receiving the news, Kgosana got half the column to wait under the pine trees at the top end of Roeland Street and diverted the other half to Caledon Square Police Station to protest against police brutality.

Police chief Colonel Terblanche and two unarmed senior policemen met the group, which Kgosana had asked to be as quiet as possible, as if they were going to a graveyard. Kgosana asked for a meeting with the Minister of Justice. Terblanche promised to arrange the meeting the next day if Kgosana would lead his group out of the city. So Kgosana rounded up the protesters and led them back to the townships without incident. That night the government declared a State of Emergency, and the police and army cordoned off the townships.

When Kgosana and two companions arrived for the meeting at Caledon Square the next morning, they were arrested. In the aftermath, Terblanche was denied any further promotion in the police force, while Kgosana escaped and went into exile. In hindsight, the combined actions of Kgosana and Terblanche potentially saved Cape Town from a major disaster.

The foundation and opening commemoration stones were both laid by Governor General Prince Arthur of Connaught. Next on the right is the **magistrates' court** ⓰, built around 1920. The next building is the 1928 **Caledon Square Police Station** ⓱. Further up on the left is the **Tafelberg Dutch Reformed Church** ⓲, built in 1892 as the Mission Hall and later converted into a Dutch Reformed church. The adjoining Cornelia House and William Frederick School were part of the original building. Up from Roeland Street, in Buitenkant Street, on the left, is the **Perseverance Tavern** ⓳, dated 1836, which claims to be the oldest pub in Cape Town. It has been modernised internally. Across the road is the beautiful **Iziko Rust en Vreugd Museum** ⓴. This was built in 1777 as a private home, and the teak veranda added 20 years later. Anreith's carvings are superb, as are the carved teak fanlights. It is arguably one of the most attractive houses in the Cape. The museum contains an interesting selection from the William Fehr Collection.

On the corner of Roeland and Buitenkant streets is the **Kimberley Hotel** ㉑, built in 1895 and reportedly one of the oldest hotels in the city. It has a typical Victorian design, crowned with a turret. On the opposite corner is **71 Roeland Street** ㉒. This attractive three-storeyed Victorian building, built circa 1900, currently houses the Book Lounge, a lively independent bookshop.

Further along Roeland Street, on the way to Parliament, is **St Mary's Cathedral** ㉓. The cathedral's foundation stone was laid in 1841. The architects were Carl Hager and C. Spaarman, and the building appears to have been the result of a joint venture. The church has 17 stained-glass windows; also noteworthy are the 14 modern paintings depicting the Stations of the Cross by South African artist Maud Sumner.

Turn left into St Johns Street. Diagonally opposite the church is the former **Belvedere Hotel** ㉔, circa 1900. Here there is a Simon van der Stel Foundation blue plaque stating that the first Jewish service in Cape town was conducted in a house on this site on 15 September 1849. Services continued until 1863, when the first synagogue was built facing Government Avenue.

The bronze statue of the Union of South Africa's first prime minister, **Louis Botha** ㉕, elected in 1910, stands on the pavement in front of the Tuynhuys.

As you walk down Plein Street, there are good views to be had of the Houses of Parliament (see page 19) from the side streets. **No. 34 Plein Street** ㉖, now Ashersons Chambers, has some art deco touches. Nos 24 and 26 used to be the premises of **W.J. Spracklen & Company** ㉗, a well-known firm of drapers and haberdashers.

Turn left into Longmarket Street and on the left is the former **Red Lion Hotel** ㉘. The building still displays the lion emblem. This was an Ohlsson's Brewery hotel that closed a number of years ago.

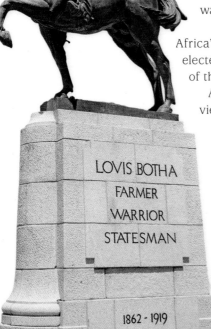

The statue of Louis Botha, first prime minister of the Union of South Africa, stands outside Tuynhuys.

LOVIS BOTHA
FARMER
WARRIOR
STATESMAN

1862 - 1919

Bo-Kaap

DISTANCE
2 km

TERRAIN
Mostly flat; some cobblestones

EFFORT
Easy, except for Longmarket Street, which is very steep and has steps

USEFUL INFORMATION

Atlas Trading Company
021 423 4361

Iziko Bo-Kaap Museum
admission charge; visitors under 18, free
021 481 3939
www.iziko.org.za

REFRESHMENTS

■ Various restaurants in Rose Street
■ Biesmiellah (restaurant and takeaway renowned for traditional Cape Malay food): Wale Street, 021 423 0850

Bo-Kaap

At the top of Wale Street, you enter a different world. The scent of spice wafts in the air and, depending on the time of day, you will hear the muezzin calling people to prayer from the mosque. The houses are colourful and have a distinctive architectural style. This is historically Cape Town's Muslim quarter. Although not exclusively populated by Muslims, their heritage has strongly influenced this neighbourhood.

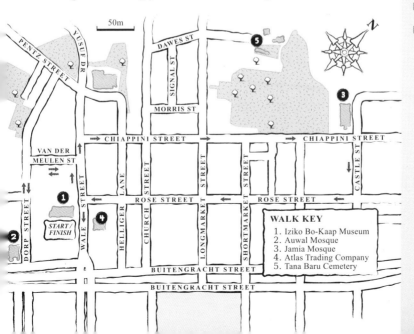

WALK KEY
1. Iziko Bo-Kaap Museum
2. Auwal Mosque
3. Jamia Mosque
4. Atlas Trading Company
5. Tana Baru Cemetery

Colourful Rose Street (above); the Iziko Bo-Kaap Museum (below)

THE WALK

Start at the **Iziko Bo-Kaap Museum ❶** at 71 Wale Street. The museum houses items and displays concerning the history and culture of Cape Town's Muslim community. The building, which features a rare wavy parapet, was erected around 1768.

The land on which it stands belonged to Jan de Waal, whose property was called Waalendorp and from whom the name Wale Street is derived. The building has a courtyard at the back, a feature that is often found in this neighbourhood. From the courtyard, stairs lead to a community hall.

From the museum, walk up Wale Street and take the arched passageway on the left through to Dorp Street. The **Auwal Mosque ❷** is reputed to be the oldest in the Cape. Its history is linked to Tuan Guru, a young Muslim holy man who arrived in the Cape in 1780.

CHOIRS AND CARNIVALS

The annual Cape Minstrel Carnival is a multi-faceted event that includes choir marches, a traditional street parade, and a string of competitions between carnival troupes, choirs and bands. It kicks of in December and usually lasts until February.

On Christmas Eve, choirs and bands parade from Bo-Kaap to the Grand Parade, where they perform a repertoire based on hymns, carols and marches. The choirs and bands come from various churches across the Cape Peninsula.

On New Year's Eve it is the turn of the *nagtroepe* (night minstrels), organised by the Cape Malay Choir Board. Traditionally, they see out the old year and usher in the New Year by marching through the city during the evening and entertaining audiences with songs and music.

The Cape Town Minstrel Carnival parade takes place on 2 January, on what is popularly known as *Tweede Nuwe Jaar* (Second New Year). This colourful event sees thousands of performers from across the city, organised into minstrel troupes, take to the streets of central Cape Town in celebration of the new year. *Tweede Nuwe Jaar* has its origins in the days of slavery, when farmers gave their slaves a day off after they had themselves celebrated New Year's Eve and New Year's Day.

The carnival spirit is extended for another two months during which the troupes compete for a number of titles at various stadiums in the city.

One of the songs that is often sung is '*Daar kom die Alabama*'. During the American Civil War, the southern confederate warship *Alabama* captured a northern ship, *Sea Bride*, in August 1863 in Table Bay, an event watched by thousands of spectators on the shore. This sea battle is commemorated in the song.

SHAEN ADEY/IOA

TANA BARU CEMETERY

The **Tana Baru Cemetery** ❺ is at the top of Longmarket Street. Walking up this steep end of the street takes some effort, but the views and the religious significance of the burial site are worth it.

Tuan Guru ('Mister Teacher') was the name given to Imam Abdullah ibn Kadi Abdus Salaam, a prince from Tidore, a small island that is part of modern-day Indonesia, who arrived at the Cape in April 1780. He was banished to the Cape for apparently backing the English in a conspiracy against the Dutch in the East Indies. On his arrival, he was imprisoned on Robben Island where he wrote down the Quran from memory. He was released in 1792 and went to live in Dorp Street in the Bo-Kaap, where he started a Muslim school, or madrasah, on the site of the Auwal Mosque.

The Jamia Mosque is also known as the Queen Victoria Mosque.

The Dutch did not allow Islam to be practised in public. In 1795, after his request for a site to build a mosque was turned down by the authorities, Tuan Guru held open-air services in a quarry on Signal Hill. During the British occupation, the restriction was relaxed and the first services were held in an old warehouse on the site of the present-day Auwal Mosque.

Tuan Guru became the city's first Imam, and is considered to be the founder of Islamic spiritual leadership in the Cape. He is famous for having written his own edition of the Quran from memory, as the authorities did not permit the Islamic holy book to be brought to the Cape. The Auwal Mosque has undergone several changes since it was first constructed.

Returning to Wale Street, walk along Chiappini Street. This is an attractive road with brightly coloured houses, mainly restored in the traditional Cape Muslim style. The side streets are worth exploring. Traditionally, the houses had one storey and were flat-roofed with parapets. Over the years, second floors were added. The area, which was close to the town centre, was initially occupied by the working classes. After slavery was abolished in 1834, more Muslims moved to the enclave, and it is estimated that by 1865 a quarter of the population of the Bo-Kaap consisted of Muslims. This proportion, as well as the number of mosques, increased over the years, which led to the area being known as the Malay Quarter.

The Boorhaanol Islam Mosque at 196 Longmarket Street was founded in 1886. On the corner of Castle and Chiappini streets is the **Jamia (Aljam) Mosque ❸**, which is also known as the Queen Victoria Mosque because the ground was granted to the Muslim community by the British Crown in 1850. The minaret above the projecting porch is dated 1932. Turn down Castle Street and then right into Rose Street to return to the starting point. A visit to the **Atlas Trading Company ❹**, opposite the museum in Wale Street, will give you a taste of the flavours and scents of this colourful suburb.

CIRCLE OF ISLAM

It is said that centuries ago it was prophesied that there would be a 'circle of Islam' in the southwestern Cape. According to local folklore, the circle protects the Cape against catastrophes. The circle comprises the kramats (burial places) of Tuan Guru and Tuan Sayeed Alawie in the Tana Baru Cemetery in Longmarket Street; the tomb of Sheikh Mohamed Hassan Ghaibie Shah, off Signal Hill Road; the grave of Sheikh Noorul Mabeen, above Victoria Road at Oudekraal; the kramat of Sayed Mahmud in Summit Road, Constantia; the kramat of Sheikh Abdurahman Matebe Shah at Klein Constantia; the shrine of Sheikh Yusuf at Macassar; and the kramat of Tuan Matarah on Robben Island.

It is traditional for a Muslim from the Cape making a pilgrimage to Mecca to visit all the shrines in the circle.

Part of the etiquette of visiting a shrine is that men and women should remove their shoes; women should cover their heads and legs; and one should show respect at the graves by avoiding loud or unnecessary conversation.

SHAEN ADEY/IOA

A typical corner shop in the Bo-Kaap

USEFUL INFORMATION

De Waal Park
open 8 a.m. till dusk

Gardens Centre
021 465 1842
www.gardensshoppingcentre.
co.za

Mount Nelson Hotel
021 483 1000
www.mountnelson.co.za

REFRESHMENTS

■ High tea at the Mount
  Nelson Hotel
■ Variety of eateries at the
  Gardens Centre

Bandstand plaque,
De Waal Park

De Waal Park entrance

De Waal Park & Gardens

This suburb of Gardens close to the Centre of Cape Town was originally part of the VOC's large vegetable garden and orchard, which supplied produce for the company's ships (see page 14). Some argue that the adjoining suburb of Oranjezicht, meaning 'orange view', got its name from the orange trees that used to

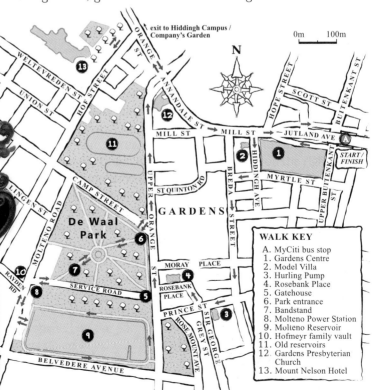

WALK KEY

A. MyCiti bus stop
1. Gardens Centre
2. Model Villa
3. Hurling Pump
4. Rosebank Place
5. Gatehouse
6. Park entrance
7. Bandstand
8. Molteno Power Station
9. Molteno Reservoir
10. Hofmeyr family vault
11. Old reservoirs
12. Gardens Presbyterian
    Church
13. Mount Nelson Hotel

grow in the VOC orchard. However, it is more likely that the name is derived from the fact that the Oranje bastion was clearly visible from the area. This is one of the five bastions of the Castle of Good Hope and is named after the Prince of Orange.

Today Gardens is a popular residential area with a mix of terrace housing and apartment blocks; a few of the gracious larger houses remain. De Waal Park provides the suburb with much-needed open space for recreation.

THE WALK

Reach the start of this walk by means of the **MyCiti bus Ⓐ** service from the city centre, which stops at the **Gardens Centre ❶**. If you choose to drive, you will find paid parking in this centre. Go past the Gardens Centre and turn left into Hiddingh Avenue. On the right is the **Model Villa ❷**, an ornate Victorian villa. At the next stop street turn right into Myrtle Street, then left into Breda Street. Continue up the slope to Prince Street, turn right and on the left is the **Hurling Pump ❸**. This is the only remaining example of the pump house system that was developed by the Burgher Council to improve Cape Town's water supply. This swing pump, built around 1795, was designed by Jan Frederick

Gardens is situated at the foot of Table Mountain, seen here with its famous 'tablecloth'.

A row of Victorian town houses, with original ironwork, lines Rosebank Place.

Hurling, a Swede who owned the Zorgvliet estate, where it was originally located. The original house, now privately owned, is obscured from view. The pump structure was designed by Louis Thibault; the lion carving is by Anton Anreith. The water was channelled to a well beneath the building. On the slate above the carving, the quantities of water used were written in chalk. Turn right into **Rosebank Place** ❹ and around the bend there are five double-storey town houses with original ironwork, including examples of broekie lace (see page 42).

Cross Upper Orange Street; opposite you is De Waal Park. The park is named after David Christiaan de Waal, a former mayor of Cape Town and a member of the Legislative Council of the Cape Colony. It was opened in 1895 and provides a pleasant green space with tree cover. Following the fence line to the left is an original **gatehouse** ❺. On the park's lower corner, where Camp Street joins Upper Orange Street, is one of the **arched metal entrances** ❻ to the park. In the centre of the park is a fountain. The **bandstand** ❼ towards the service road was built by Walter Macfarlane of Glasgow and erected for the Great Exhibition at Green Point Common in 1904–1905, before being reconstructed in its current position. An active Friends of De Waal Park Association raises funds for amenities and services in the park. Summer concerts are held here at weekends. Exiting onto Molteno Road, turn left and you will see the **Molteno Power Station** ❽, the first hydroelectric power station in the country, opened in 1894 as the Graaff Electric Light Works. The **Molteno Reservoir** ❾ was completed in 1886 after a leak caused flooding to surrounding houses, which delayed its construction. It is possible to walk along Belvedere Avenue to Upper Orange Street, but a more attractive route is back through the park. There is a **vault** of the **Hofmeyr family** ❿ on Molteno Road, opposite the service road to the park. Opposite the park off Camp Street are the **old reservoirs** ⓫, dating from 1852. On the corner of Upper Orange Street and Orange Street is the **Gardens Presbyterian Church** ⓬ designed by architect John Parker and built in 1902. To visit the **Mount Nelson Hotel** ⓭, turn left into Orange Street and left again through the grand pillared archway. From here, return to the Gardens Centre along Orange Street.

MOUNT NELSON HOTEL

In the late nineteenth century the Castle-Line shipping company felt that a top-class hotel was needed for its first-class passengers. In 1890 Sir Donald Currie, chairman of the company, acquired a magnificent property at the top end of Government Avenue (opposite the Company's Garden). The hotel was designed by London architects Dunn & Watson, who appointed Herbert Baker as the supervising architect. The London building firm Cubbits was the contractor. When the Mount Nelson Hotel opened in 1899, it was the first hotel in South Africa to have hot and cold running water in the rooms. The establishment was extended in 1921, when an impressive pillared gateway was added at the bottom of Palm Avenue. The five-star hotel is set back from Orange Street in attractive gardens. The original paintwork was pale yellow and green, which was changed to ochre and red; in 1923 the distinctive pink, its current colour, was applied.

During the Anglo-Boer War, the hotel became the informal officers' mess of the British Army. Lord Roberts and General Kitchener often stayed there, as did Winston Churchill when he was a young correspondent covering the war.

Over 100 years later, this luxury hotel has an international reputation and clientele, and is popular with visitors and locals alike. It is renowned for the high tea served daily in the elegant lounge.

DISTANCE
2,5 km

TERRAIN
Flat; slight slope
to the time-ball
tower

EFFORT
Easy

USEFUL INFORMATION

Chavonnes Battery Museum
admission charge; discounts
for children and pensioners
021 416 6230
www.chavonnesmuseum.co.za

Iziko Maritime Centre
admission charge;
visitors under 18, free
021 405 2880
www.iziko.org

Nelson Mandela Gateway
for bookings to
Robben Island
www.robbenisland.org.za

Two Oceans Aquarium
various discounts for children,
depending on age
021 418 3823
www.aquarium.co.za

V&A Waterfront
021 408 7500
www.waterfront.co.za

REFRESHMENTS

■ Dozens of food options,
including a food court
■ Den Anker, for good
Belgian food and great
views of Table Mountain:
021 419 0249, www.
denankerrestaurant.co.za

Alfred Basin

V&A Waterfront

The development of the V&A Waterfront around the Alfred Basin, which began in 1989 at the Pierhead, has brought the public close to the harbour once again. Today the Waterfront, as well as being part of an attractive working harbour, is an exciting and interesting destination for visitors. The larger, modern Duncan Dock, developed between 1937 and 1943, is mostly closed to the public for security reasons.

The Waterfront offers prime shopping, world-class hotels, and an extensive range of restaurants, cafés and entertainment areas, providing a vibrant environment for visitors and locals alike.

It is possible to visit the Waterfront by using the MyCiti bus system or by water taxi along the canal from the Cape Town International Convention Centre.

THE WALK

Adjacent to the amphitheatre outside the Victoria Wharf Shopping Centre is the old Union-Castle Building. Start at the **wall map ❶** in the passage next to this building. The map shows the old shoreline and the position of the VOC forts and subsequent defences. It also illustrates how the reclamation of the Foreshore (see page 36) created Duncan Dock and the infill of Woodstock Beach formed the container basin.

It took over 200 years and severe loss of ships during strong north-westerly storms before plans were made for a safe harbour to be built at the Cape. This was at the behest of Cape governor Sir George Grey. The key to the harbour was the excavation of a basin, which provided stone to build a breakwater. It was an expensive scheme and convict labour was used to keep down the costs. The governor persuaded the British Parliament to finance the project and he got the support of the Eastern Cape government representatives, who had originally wanted the harbour to be in Port Elizabeth or East London. He also had the idea of inviting Queen Victoria's son, Prince Alfred, a 15-year-old midshipman, to tip the first stones for the breakwater. At the entrance to the shopping centre, on the side of the amphitheatre, there is a **plaque** ❷ commemorating this event. It is reported that, on 17 September 1860, 20 000 people (out of a population of 33 000) attended the ceremony, at which both Prince Alfred and Sir George Grey spoke.

This plaque marks the start of construction on the breakwater.

Walk towards the **Victoria & Alfred Hotel** ❸, with Quay 4 on the left, and follow the road around the hotel to the left until you face the corner of the Alfred Basin. At first the stone for the basin was quarried out of the ground and taken by horse and cart to

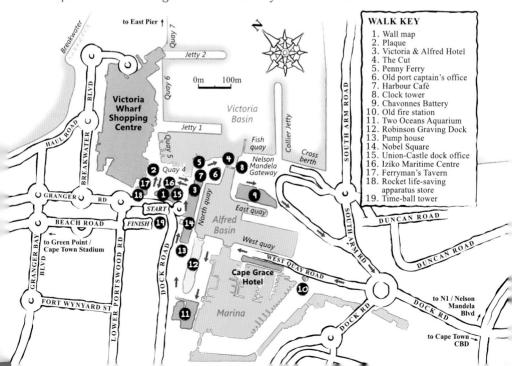

WALK KEY

1. Wall map
2. Plaque
3. Victoria & Alfred Hotel
4. The Cut
5. Penny Ferry
6. Old port captain's office
7. Harbour Café
8. Clock tower
9. Chavonnes Battery
10. Old fire station
11. Two Oceans Aquarium
12. Robinson Graving Dock
13. Pump house
14. Nobel Square
15. Union-Castle dock office
16. Iziko Maritime Centre
17. Ferryman's Tavern
18. Rocket life-saving apparatus store
19. Time-ball tower

The old port captain's office was built in 1904.

the breakwater. By 1861 the convict workforce had grown to 858 prisoners. A prison (Breakwater Prison on Portswood Ridge) had been built to accommodate them. In 1863 a steam locomotive replaced the horses and a steam crane was used to lift heavy blocks. Nitroglycerine replaced gunpowder for blasting in 1886.

The entrance to the Alfred Basin was known as the Cut.

Walk along the harbour past Den Anker Restaurant and turn left towards the entrance to the Alfred Basin, originally known as **the Cut** ❹. The basin was opened in 1869, and its breakwater was 550 metres long. Prince Alfred, then the Duke of Edinburgh, returned to the Cape in 1870 to officially open the Alfred Basin. Sailing ships were 'warped' through the Cut and towed in and out of the basin until they could get a favourable wind in the bay. Warping involved towing the vessels by ropes that were run through guide sheaves on the edge of the quay to windlasses and bollards fastened to the quayside. This equipment is still in position today.

A windlass was used to pull sailing ships through the Cut.

Before you go over the bridge, on the Victoria Basin side, you will see a flight of steps going down to the water. In 1871 a rowing boat began to be used to ferry staff across the entrance of the Alfred Basin. When the ferry service opened to the general public in 1880, passengers were charged a penny for the passage, and it soon became known as the **Penny Ferry** ❺. To the right of the steps, the imposing three-storey building is the **old port captain's office** ❻, built in 1904. The double-storey building on the right is the old **Harbour Café** ❼. Erected in 1903, this has been used as a tea room and, at one stage, a post office.

THE OLD SHORELINE

In 1860 the sea came up to the Castle of Good Hope. With the development of the first railway station and the pier, the sea was reclaimed to the line of the Esplanade, a promenade that used to run along the shore, past the pier towards Woodstock on one side and the Alfred Basin on the other.

In 1920 the pier was where the fountain at the bottom of Adderley Street is today. On the Sea Point side of the city, Dock Road ran from Adderley Street through to the old harbour. Today Jetty Street, off Lower Long Street, and the North Wharf Square, at the bottom of Loop Street, recall the fishing boats and the fish market at Roggebaai. Interpretation boards in the square explain some of the history and there is a wooden replica of part of the jetty.

The only remaining historical building on the shoreside of Dock Road is the Spearhead Building, formerly the Imperial Cold Storage Building, which was built in 1896. In the Victorian entrance foyer is a mural of a map of Table Bay and a large panoramic photograph of Cape Town taken circa 1914.

On the corner of Alfred Street, at the entrance to the V&A Waterfront, is a small cobbled section of Dock Road. The building on the corner used to be the Queen's Hotel (the name is visible on the pediment). Around the corner in Port Road are the remains of the Amsterdam Battery, built in 1781 as part of the VOC's seaward defence line.

Cross over the Cut on the new swing bridge. The Gothic-style **clock tower** ❽ was originally known as the Dock Clock and the Tide Gauge Tower. It was used as the port captain's office. On the second floor is the mirror room, which allowed the port captain to see all around the harbour. The clock was made by J.A. Ritchie & Sons of Edinburgh. On the Alfred Basin side is part of the **Chavonnes Battery** ❾, named after Lieutenant Colonel Mauritz de Chavonnes, a governor of the Cape in the eighteenth century. Built by slave labour, the battery was extended over the years and became a fort with cannons on different levels. Other forts in the Cape included Fort Knokke (1743) in Woodstock; Imhoff, in front of the Castle; the Amsterdam Battery, near the City Lodge entrance to the Waterfront (1787); and Kyk in die Pot (1795) near the Mouille Point Battery. The royal salute for Prince Alfred was fired from the ramparts of the Chavonnes Battery in 1860, and in 1884 the battery was used as an isolation unit during a smallpox epidemic. It was partly demolished to allow construction of the harbour. In 1999 an archaeological dig found the remains of the fort. The museum gives the history of the period.

Beyond the clock tower is the Clock Tower Centre. A viewing platform next to the Nelson Mandela Gateway offers an expansive view across Victoria Basin. The first quay on the right is Collier Jetty. Irvin & Johnson operates its deep-sea fishing fleet from Cross Jetty. Carl Johnson, a Swede, teamed up with G.D. Irvin to form Atlantic Whaling in 1890. With the advent of cold storage, they moved into fishing and by 1906 there was a weekly 'fish train' service operating with refrigerated trucks between Cape Town and Johannesburg.

Victoria Basin evolved as a result of the extension of the breakwater. The south arm

The Gothic-style clock tower was built in 1882. Its trademark red colour was temporarily changed to yellow, the brand colour of Cape Town's successful bid for selection as the 2014 World Design Capital.

ROBBEN ISLAND

In the middle of Table Bay, buffeted in summer by the Cape's southeaster and in winter by the north-west gales, is a lonely island. The name was given by the Dutch because of the large number of seals (*robben* in Dutch) found there.

Jan van Riebeeck visited the island in 1653 and used it as a pantry, collecting penguin eggs and keeping sheep there. He also banished to the island criminals and political prisoners from the Dutch East Indies. Slate tiles were quarried there and used in the construction of the Castle and other buildings. The island was used as a penal settlement, and from 1845 as a leper colony. The lighthouse was built around 1865 on the highest point, Minto Hill. There is a small village consisting of the Anglican Church, built in 1841, and a few Victorian houses, some used by the Robben Island staff.

From 1931, it ceased to be used as a leper colony. From the start of World War II, navy and military personnel were stationed there. A large gun emplacement helped guard the bay. The navy remained until 1965, when the Department of Prisons took over the island and housed thousands of mainly political prisoners, including Nelson Mandela and Robert Sobukwe, in the high-security prison. The kramat of Tuan Matarah, a Muslim holy man who was exiled there in the mid-eighteenth century, is on Robben Island (see also Circle of Islam, page 61).

Guided tours of the island must be booked in advance from the Nelson Mandela Gateway in the V&A Waterfront.

was used exclusively by the British Navy during the Anglo-Boer War. At its busiest, the port accommodated 111 vessels in one day – 35 in the docks and 76 at anchor in the roadstead. On 2 February 1901, there was an outbreak of bubonic plague caused by rats among bales of forage imported from Argentina. There were 619 cases reported and 300 people died. The 1 500 black labourers who lived at the harbour were moved to Uitvlugt, later known as Ndabeni, near Pinelands.

Work started on the Duncan Dock in 1937 and it was completed in 1943. It is named after Sir Patrick Duncan, who was the first South African to be appointed governor general, from 1936 to 1943. Many Capetonians regretted the demolition of the Cape Town pier to make way for this redevelopment. A Dutch contractor dredged the seabed to create the harbour, and the sand and mud were used to form the 194-hectare site of reclaimed land called the Foreshore.

The walk continues around the slipway where small ships are cleaned and painted. Walk along West Quay Road. On the left, before the Cape Grace Hotel, is a small building with a large arched doorway. Originally, this was the first **fire station** ⑩ housed in the harbour. Later it fulfilled another important function when it became the office of the rat catcher. Behind the hotel is the newly opened small-craft basin. This used to be the quarry where stone for constructing the Victoria Basin breakwater was obtained. From the early 1920s, it was used as a storage depot for petrol.

ANTHONY JOHNSON/IOA

Nearby, in Dock Road, is the **Two Oceans Aquarium** ⑪. Built in 1995, it features a shark tank, diving experiences and a wide variety of aquatic species found in the southern oceans.

The **Robinson Graving Dock** ⑫ was named after Sir Hercules Robinson, a governor of the Cape. It was opened in October 1882. The dry dock was used for swimming galas before the Long Street Baths were built. The caisson is floated into place once the ship is in the dry dock. The caisson is then filled with water and the water pumped out of the dry dock. Note the old cannons around the dry dock entrance, which are used as bollards. The **pump house** ⑬ is still in use today and was originally attached to the power station. On 25 April 1882, the first electric lights were switched on. The power station also provided electricity to operate the pump house, the old part of the Somerset Hospital and the Houses of Parliament.

The Two Oceans Aquarium has extensive displays of the prolific sea life of the southern oceans.

The statues in Nobel Square pay tribute to South Africa's four Nobel Peace Prize laureates.

In **Nobel Square** ⑭ there is a display of four sculptures by Claudette Schreuders. The bronze artworks honour South Africa's four Nobel Peace Prize laureates: Albert Luthuli (1960); Desmond Tutu (1984); and F.W. de Klerk and Nelson Mandela (both in 1993). In front of them is a sculpture to peace, democracy and non-violence by Noria Mabasa, an artist from Limpopo.

Walk past the **Union-Castle dock office** ⑮, which was built in 1919 by Baker, Kendal & Morris Architects. The lucrative mail-delivery contract between South Africa and Britain was a highly sought-after arrangement for shipping companies. The Union Steamship Company and the Castle Mail Packer Company merged in 1900 to form the Union-Castle Line. The **Iziko Maritime Centre** ⑯ is on the first floor and has models of passenger ships used on the Cape route. It also has an extensive research library.

Walk towards the Victoria Wharf Shopping Centre and turn left towards the Portswood Ridge. On the right is the **Ferryman's Tavern** ⑰, the oldest warehouse in the docks, dating from 1873. Past it on the right is the site of the old **Rocket life-saving apparatus store** ⑱. When there was a shipwreck, a rocket projectile was attached to a rope that was fired onto the vessel and used to winch survivors ashore. This was last used at the wreck of the SA *Seafarer* in 1966, after which helicopters were recognised as the most efficient rescue vessels (see page 85). On the way up to the Portswood Ridge is the entrance to the tunnel through which the wagons ran that carried stone to the breakwater.

The **time-ball tower** ⑲ was opened in 1894 and built up to double its original height in 1903. This device was used for synchronising the time for ships – essential before modern navigation equipment came into use. Knowing the correct time was important in determining longitude. Nearby, the harbour

UNION-CASTLE LINE

In February 1900, the shareholders of the Union Line and Sir Donald Currie's Castle Line agreed to the amalgamation of the two shipping firms. The livery of the new company, the Union-Castle Line, was a lavender-coloured hull and red-and-black-topped funnels. The mail ships sailed weekly between Cape Town and England, a 14-day voyage. The communication link with Britain included mail, newspapers and magazines, and important documents and cargo that needed the fastest passage possible. The line also provided a passenger service.

In 1938 the mail service started, but was interrupted by the outbreak of World War II. During the war, the ships were requisitioned to serve in a variety of capacities, including armed merchant cruisers, escort aircraft carriers, hospital ships and troop ships.

In 1948 the regular weekly mail service recommenced, with ships covering the 5 978 nautical miles from Southampton to Cape Town in 13½ days. They also ran a 10-day coastal voyage to Durban, which was popular with South Africans. The line provided an intermediate service up the east coast, as well as a round-Africa service, both of which served the movement of officials in the British Colonial Service.

The introduction of a 747 airline service by South African Airways in 1971 and a regular, fast container-ship service made the cost of running passenger vessels unviable, and on 6 September 1977, the *Windsor Castle* sailed for the last time from Cape Town, ending a long-standing service.

master's house has been converted into a hotel. On Portswood Road is the old Breakwater Prison, a site also used as a hotel (see page 83) and as UCT's Graduate School of Business.

Look down from the Portswood Ridge and you will see the Victoria & Alfred Hotel, which was converted from the North Quay warehouse. Quay 4, where the National Sea Rescue Institute boat is stationed, was once used for boat building. Beyond that, Quay 5 was used for small coasters. At the end of the quay, the prison boats sailed to Robben Island.

The view from atop the ridge provides an overall perspective on the old harbour and how it has been extended and modified to become one of the most successful working-harbour developments in the world.

The time-ball tower on Portswood Ridge was used to synchronise time for ships.

USEFUL INFORMATION

Cape Quarter Lifestyle Centre
021 421 1111
www.capequarter.co.za

Prestwich Memorial
021 487 2755

REFRESHMENTS

- Cape Quarter Lifestyle Centre (restaurants, toilets, shops)
- Coffee shop at Prestwich Memorial (entrance from St Andrew's Square)

A war memorial at St Andrew's Church, off Waterkant Street

De Waterkant

Fan Walk

During the 2010 FIFA™ Soccer World Cup, which South Africa hosted, an innovative plan was devised to move thousands of people from the Grand Parade in the city centre to the Cape Town Stadium at Green Point. The route was closed to traffic on match days and entertainers in the form of drummers, minstrel singers and fire-eaters lined the way. Restaurants and bars spilled onto the pavement and a jovial spirit prevailed.

The route has been designed to start at the railway station in Adderley Street and end at the Cape Quarter Lifestyle Centre on Somerset Road, as there is not a lot to see between there and the stadium further on. Alternatively, you could start at the Cape Quarter and do a circular walk, to Long Street and back.

THE WALK

From Cape Town Station, cross Adderley Street and walk up Waterkant Street. In 1790 this street was on the seashore and as the shore silted up in the nineteenth century, the town expanded by adding the next street, Riebeek Street.

After crossing Long Street, you reach Sea Street. Its name indicates its former proximity to the shoreline, before the reclamation of land along the Foreshore. A couple of converted warehouses still exist in this lane.

No. 24, on the corner of Loop Street, dates from around 1900. The three-storey building has a cast-iron veranda by Macfarlane of Glasgow; the third floor has a corner turret.

The date 'Est. 1884' on Nos 35–37 refers to the original single-storey building; the additional floors have a date of 1900. Note the attic windows.

No. 43, the Crow Bar, used to have a live bird in a cage, but this is gone. The building has an ornate pediment circa 1900. The next three buildings have different pediment styles.

No. 45 was built circa 1900 with a rounded gable, whereas No. 47, built circa 1910, has a triangular pediment. No. 49 is from around the same period as the others and has a plaster parapet. On the right, at the corner of Waterkant and Bree streets, the building is unnumbered but dates from 1910. No. 48 is an attractive two-storey Victorian building with a centre parapet marked 'established in 1887'.

No. 50 is a narrow two-storey with the name 'Pailley and Jocum', circa 1900. No. 52 is a two-storey house embellished with cast-iron Victorian features, circa 1895. No. 54 is a three-storey with a Gothic-style gable and some Edwardian touches. Further on, No. 56, Tramway House, is dated 1905.

A pedestrian bridge, built as part of the Fan Walk, spans the busy Buitengracht Street and there is a

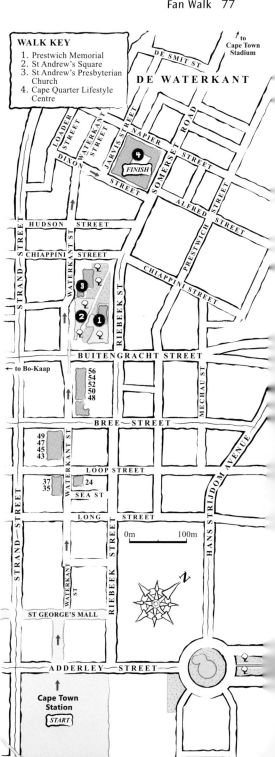

WALK KEY
1. Prestwich Memorial
2. St Andrew's Square
3. St Andrew's Presbyterian Church
4. Cape Quarter Lifestyle Centre

The Greek temple-style facade of St Andrew's Church (above); display board at the Prestwich Memorial (below)

pedestrian/cycle traffic light if you wish to avoid the stairs of the bridge. Buitengracht was the edge of the town during the VOC period. The area towards Green Point Common used to be a semi-wasteland, with cemeteries and the city's gallows.

The **Prestwich Memorial** ❶ contains an ossuary that holds the remains of people who were buried outside the formal burial grounds. Slaves, shipwreck victims and indigenous people were likely to have been buried here. Outside, a remnant of the original Dutch Reformed Church cemetery wall is displayed. There is also a memorial garden.

In **St Andrew's Square** ❷ a small section of tram tracks is visible. The horse-drawn tram ran along Somerset Road (named after Lord Charles Somerset, governor from 1814–1820) on its route to Sea Point. The **St Andrew's Presbyterian Church** ❸ was built in 1827/8. It was designed by Henry William Reveley. The former rectory adjoining the church was built in the Georgian period.

Waterkant Street leads into the small, quaint area known as De Waterkant. It stretches from Loader Street to Somerset Road, and its boundaries are Dixon and De Smit streets. The area developed from around the 1830s and was made up of mainly small dwellings. The neighbourhood was affected by the Group Areas Act and many of its residents were forced to move in 1966. The vacant houses were purchased and renovated by white speculators. While some of the streetscapes were retained, additional storeys and roof decks were added, and a variety of architectural styles appeared. The restaurants, shops and offices of the new **Cape Quarter Lifestyle Centre** ❹ on Somerset Road have introduced a more commercial element to the neighbourhood – but the area still retains a certain charm. Some of the facades of the old warehouse buildings in Somerset Road have been incorporated into the Cape Quarter development.

Green Point Urban Park

DISTANCE
3 km

TERRAIN
Flat

EFFORT
Easy; there can
be strong winds

Green Point

The land at Green Point, adjacent to central Cape Town, was originally granted to Jan van Riebeeck in the seventeenth century. The name comes from the fact that the abundant water in the area keeps the vegetation green all year round. Van Riebeeck tried to grow wheat here but the strong winds damaged the crops. He exchanged this grant for Bosch Heuwel Farm, on the slopes of Wynberg Hill.

Over the years, **Green Point Common ❶** has been used as a pasture for dairy cows, a lake for boating and fishing, a military camp and a British prisoner-of-war camp. It has been home to several sports clubs and provided an athletic and cycling track. Horse racing in Cape Town has its origins here, and it has been the venue for recreational events, exhibitions, fairs and circuses.

USEFUL INFORMATION

Breakwater Lodge Hotel
021 406 1911
www.proteahotels.com/breakwaterlodge

Cape Medical Museum
admission charge
021 418 5663

Fort Wynyard
although not officially open to the public, a visit can be arranged if requested in advance
021 419 1765

Green Point Lighthouse
admission charge
021 449 5172

REFRESHMENTS

- Picnic facilities in the Urban Park
- Pepenero Italian & Seafood Restaurant (along the beach front): 021 439 9027, www.pepenero.co.za
- Wafu and Wakame Asian Fusion (along the beach front): 021 433 2377, www.wakame.co.za

WALK KEY

A. MyCiti bus stop
1. Green Point Common
2. Urban Park
3. Green Point Lighthouse
4. Old Turf Club Building (McDonald's)
5. Cape Town Stadium
6. Fort Wynyard
7. Cape Medical Museum
8. Breakwater Lodge Hotel
9. Somerset Hospital
10. RMS *Athens*

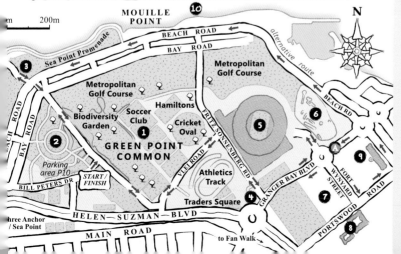

After years of semi-neglect and underuse, this recreational area has been given a new lease of life as a result of the new stadium that was built for the 2010 FIFA™ Soccer World Cup. Adjacent to Green Point Common is the **Green Point Urban Park ❷**, which was designed to coincide with the opening of the stadium in 2010. This park has transformed an unattractive area into an educational and interactive asset, which is used and enjoyed by people of all ages.

THE WALK

Start at the gate into the Urban Park next to the P10 parking area. This is well signposted from Helen Suzman Boulevard. The main walkway runs on an axis with the **Green Point Lighthouse ❸**. It is also possible to take the **MyCiti bus ❹** to Granger Bay Boulevard and walk the route from there to the Urban Park.

Green Point Lighthouse was built in 1824; the foghorn is known to locals as Moaning Minnie.

If you have started at the gate to the Urban Park, walk across Bay and Beach roads to the lighthouse, which was

SHAEN ADEY/IOA

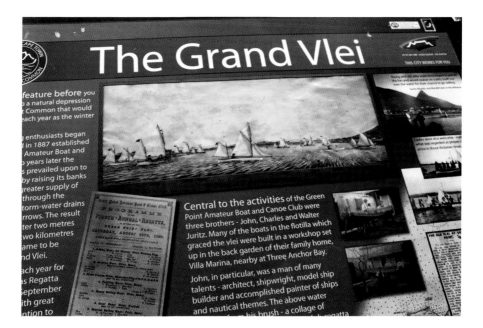

opened in 1824. The builder was Herman Schutte, who built the Groote Kerk in Adderley Street (see page 26). The base of the building is unaltered but the tower has been heightened and it was electrified in 1929. The foghorn was introduced in 1926, much to the annoyance of some of the neighbours, and still sounds its warning on foggy days.

The information boards at the Green Point Urban Park give a brief history of the area.

In the Urban Park there are tables and benches for the public to enjoy picnics while children play in the modern playground nearby. The biodiversity garden has attractive indigenous plants and informative signboards. The water used in the garden and the park is piped from a perennial stream.

The Metropolitan Golf Club has had its course redesigned and reconfigured, and provides an attractive border on one side. The city's Heritage Department has placed a number of illustrated interpretation boards describing the historical background of the activities that have taken place here over the years. There was a sailing club on the old Green Point Vlei. The first horse races were held on the common and the building that now houses McDonald's was built by the **South African Turf Club** ➍ in 1851, and contained a small grandstand and offices. It is much altered but retains some of its Georgian dignity. At one stage, it was used as the clubhouse of the Metropolitan Golf Club.

The **Cape Town Stadium** ❺, which opened in 2010, has a seating capacity of 55 000. Next door, a state-of-the art athletics stadium was completed in 2013. During the Anglo-Boer War (1899–1902), the area was taken over by the British Army, and from March 1900 it was the site of a prisoner-of-war camp for Boer prisoners. Adjacent to this camp was a second facility used for Boer prisoners who were about to be deported to British concentration camps. It was known as Skyview because it was surrounded by a high corrugated fence, affording views of only the sky.

In 1904/5 the Great Cape Town Exhibition was held on the Green Point Common. Exhibition Building on Main Road and a small adjoining street, Exhibition Terrace, recall this event.

In the shadow of the Cape Town Stadium is the Green Point Memorial Wall.

Walk down Granger Bay Boulevard. On the left is **Fort Wynyard** ❻, which was built in 1862 on the site of the VOC's Kyk in die Pot fort, which was demolished in 1827. It is on a slight hill and overlooks the bay. It is now used as an artillery museum and is part of the Cape Garrison Artillery. The fort is named after R.H. Wynyard, a lieutenant general of the Cape Colony. The statue of the Lady of Hope is displayed at the fort This figure was also depicted on the cap badge of the South African Cape Corps. There are muzzleloaders and cannons dating from 1846, as well as guns that were part of the defences during World Wars I and II. Of special interest are the building known as the Long Gallery and a system of tunnels. Also in the complex is the Green Point

Green Point Memorial Wall • Groenpunt-gedenkmuur • UDonga olusiSikhumbuzo IwaseGreen Point

Memorial Wall, which commemorates the Boer prisoners of war who died here during the Anglo-Boer War of 1899–1902.

Walk along Fort Wynyard Road towards Cape Town. On the right is the **Cape Medical Museum ❼**. This Victorian villa was formerly the residence of the medical superintendent of the Hospital for Infectious Diseases. It houses an interesting collection of early medical equipment and memorabilia that reveals the medical history of the early days of the Cape.

Across Portswood Road, the old Breakwater Prison, now the **Breakwater Lodge Hotel ❽**, was built as the new convict station between 1895 and 1901 to house the labour force used to build the harbour. It was converted in 1992 to accommodate a hotel and UCT's Graduate School of Business. A grim reminder of its previous life is the treadmill that stands in the grounds, and the row of condemned cells nearby.

The statue of the Lady of Hope, Fort Wynyard

Turn left down Portswood Road. On the corner of Beach Road is the **Somerset Hospital ❾**. The memorial stone was laid in 1859. This castle-like building with its simulated battlements overlooks the Waterfront. The drinking fountain in the front was erected by the citizens of Cape Town to mark the visit of the Duke and Duchess of Cornwall on 20 August 1901. The previous Somerset Hospital, since demolished, was in Hospital Street, below Somerset Road. Retrace your steps to the starting point or, if you wish, continue to the V&A Waterfront (see page 66).

Alternatively, you can return to the starting point by walking along Beach Road and the beach front, with views across the sea to Robben Island. This will extend your walk by another two kilometres. Along the rocks in Mouille Point are the remains of the **RMS *Athens* ❿**, wrecked during the great gale of 17 May 1765. She tried to steam out of Table Bay but heavy seas extinguished her boiler fires and she was wrecked on the rocks. All on board perished except, so it is said, for a pig which made its way ashore! The ship's engine block is still visible. This part of the route offers more choice of cafés and restaurants.

DISTANCE
2,5 km

TERRAIN
Flat

EFFORT
Easy

USEFUL INFORMATION

Sea Point Swimming Pool
021 434 3341

Winchester Mansions Hotel
021 434 2351

REFRESHMENTS

- Kiosks at Sea Point Swimming Pool or eateries along the beach front
- La Perla, on the corner of St John's Road and Beach Road, is an old, established Italian restaurant: 021 434 2471, www.laperla.co.za
- Winchester Mansions Hotel: 021 434 2351, www.winchester.co.za

Beach Road

Sea Point

The area between Lion's Head and the Atlantic was named by Samuel Wallis, one of Captain Cook's commanders, in 1776, when he encamped his ship's company 'at the point next to the sea' to escape the smallpox epidemic raging in Cape Town. Over the years, the City Council has preserved the wide grassed area between Three Anchor Bay and

WALK KEY

1. Winchester Mansions Hotel
2. Hall Road Station plaque
3. Drinking fountain
4. Milton Road Station plaque
5. Sea Point Swimming Pool
6. Tidal pool
7. Graaff's Pool
8. White Horses sculpture
9. Outdoor gymnasium
10. Three Anchor Bay Station plaque
11. Geological Exposure

GILLIAN BLACK

the swimming pool. In many cities around the world, such land has often been sold off to make way for restaurants and other lucrative enterprises. The lawn offers a recreational space for children and adults, residents and people from further afield.

In the early 1900s, Beach Road was fronted by grand Victorian houses with large gardens. By the early 1950s, there were seven licensed and eight private hotels along the beach front. Some of the names of the original establishments have been retained by the apartment blocks that have replaced them.

The elegant Winchester Mansions Hotel in Sea Point

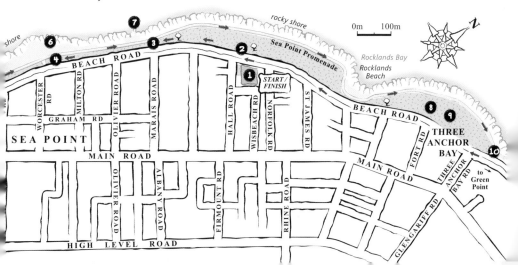

These plaques recall the era when Sea Point had a railway line.

THE WALK

Start at the **Winchester Mansions Hotel ❶** on Beach Road – a well-known landmark. Originally built as apartments in the 1920s, the building was converted into a hotel in the 1950s. It has an attractive covered central courtyard.

Cross Beach Road at the pedestrian traffic light. Opposite the hotel is a **commemorative plaque ❷** marking the site of Hall Road Station. Surprising as it may seem, a railway line ran from near Cape Town Station to near where the Sea Point Swimming Pool is today. The first company, the Metropolitan and Suburban Railway Company, started in 1892. It used a steam train that traversed the Green Point Common. The line closed in 1898.

There were nine stations – Monument, Ebenezer Road, Cycle Track, Pine Grove, Three Anchor Bay, Hall Road, Milton Road, Clarens Road and Sea Point. It was reopened by the Cape Government Railway in 1905. It was electrified in 1927 and finally closed in 1929.

Continue on the pavement in the direction of the swimming pool. On the lawn opposite Marais Road is a **drinking fountain ❸** for dogs and their owners. This unusual amenity was donated to the people of Sea Point in 2012

RESCUE OF SA *SEAFARER*

On 1 July 1966, in the early morning, the SA *Seafarer*, with a crew of 63 and 12 passengers, ran aground in heavy seas opposite the Green Point Lighthouse. Attempts to connect lines to the ship by rocket launchers failed and the port captain called on the air force at Ysterplaat for help. Three Alouette helicopters were sent to airlift the passengers and crew ashore. The lighthouse centred its beam on the ship to help the personnel in the operation. It was the first time a sea–air rescue operation was performed in South Africa.

The ship was a wreck and some of its cargo, which included a consignment of White Horse Whisky, was washed ashore. After high tide, whisky bottles were found embedded in the sand at angles similar to those now portrayed in a public art installation of white horses along the Sea Point promenade.

A fortuitous spin-off from the wreck is that chemicals leaking from the hold killed off dense kelp growth that had covered a much older wreck – the *Vis* (1740), a wooden vessel wrecked nearby – which enabled divers to recover coins from the older ship.

by an English couple who spent part of the Cape summer here. At Milton Road there is another **plaque** ❹ marking the site of the station on the old railway.

Upon reaching the outdoor public **Sea Point Swimming Pool** ❺, cross to the promenade. There is access to the beach here, and at Milton Road the **tidal pool** ❻ is ideal for children. Further along, **Graaff's Pool** ❼ was originally for men only and nude bathing used to be allowed. The pool was created when rock was excavated from here for use in railway foundations. The height of the screening wall has since been reduced.

At Three Anchor Bay, a group of five small **white horses** ❽, placed at odd angles, forms a play-and-listen area. This sculpture commemorates a significant sea-rescue operation (see 'Rescue of SA *Seafarer*' on page 86).

Nearby is an **outdoor gymnasium** ❾. Back on the Beach Road pavement is a **plaque** ❿ that marks the position of the old Three Anchor Bay Station. Return to the Winchester Mansions Hotel, whose pleasant terrace overlooks the sea.

GEOLOGICAL EXPOSURE

As you head towards the end of Sea Point from the swimming pool, a three-kilometre return walk along the coast will take you to the Geological Exposure ⓫ (or Sea Point Contact), near Saunders Rocks, where the dark Malmesbury shale contrasts with the pale Cape granite. Charles Darwin visited this spot in 1836 when he came to the Cape on the HMS *Beagle*, which was circumnavigating the southern hemisphere.

Sea Point Swimming Pool is a popular spot during summer.

DISTANCE
± 2,5 km

TERRAIN
Flat; steep slope
to cannons

EFFORT
Moderate

USEFUL INFORMATION

Bay Hotel (Rotunda)
021 430 4444
www.thebayhotel.com

Roundhouse
021 438 4347

Theatre on the Bay
021 438 3301
info@theatreonthebay.co.za

REFRESHMENTS
Large choice of cafés and
restaurants on Victoria Road
along the beach front

Victoria Road

Camps Bay

South of Sea Point are the fashionable seaside resorts of Bantry Bay and Clifton. Beyond Clifton and its famous four beaches is palm-tree-lined Camps Bay. A few decades ago, this was a sleepy village with a few shops, including a chemist and a grocery store … and a resident white horse called Philly who used to munch the grass of the local soccer field.

In the last 40 years or so, Camps Bay has grown into a busy, cosmopolitan seaside resort where every available space has been developed.

The cannons on Lower Kloof Road were placed there by the Dutch in 1782.

THE WALK

Start at the **cannons** ❶ on Lower Kloof Road, below Camps Bay School. This fortification was erected by the Dutch in 1782. There was concern that Camps Bay Beach would provide a possible landing site if the Cape were invaded by a foreign power. As you look back towards Cape Town, you can see the Clifton Scenic Reserve stretching down to the sea from Victoria Road. Another area of natural vegetation runs up from Victoria Road, across Kloof Road and onto the slopes of the Lion's Head. This gives you an idea of what the area looked like before the intensive building development took place.

Victoria Road, named after the British queen, was built as the coast road from Sea Point by road engineer Thomas Bain. The extension of the route south to Hout Bay was completed in 1888.

As you come down the slope to Victoria Road, look out for the two metal pole bases next to the stone retaining wall along the pavement. These were **poles** ❷ that supported the tram cables for the Camps Bay Tramways Company.

In 1900 a syndicate was formed to develop Camps Bay as a residential area. To facilitate convenient transport access, a tram system was envisaged, running from Cape Town to Camps Bay Beach. The syndicate bought all the vacant land, mainly farmland, in Camps Bay between the sea and the mountain, and had it subdivided into building plots. In 1901 three companies were registered – the Camps Bay Tramways Company, Oranjezicht Estates Company and Cape Marine Suburbs Limited. In November 1901, the first tram made the journey along Kloof Road to the beach front at Camps Bay. The secretary of the company was James

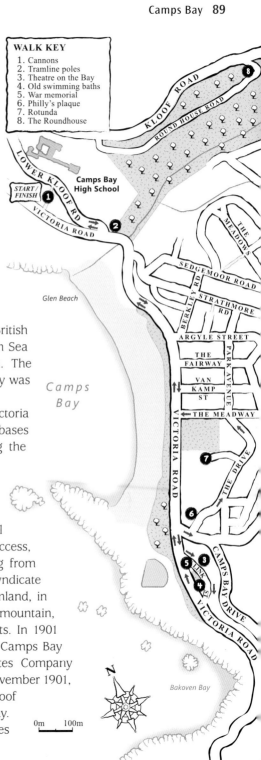

WALK KEY
1. Cannons
2. Tramline poles
3. Theatre on the Bay
4. Old swimming baths
5. War memorial
6. Philly's plaque
7. Rotunda
8. The Roundhouse

Camps Bay High School

START / FINISH ❶

Glen Beach

Camps Bay

Bakoven Bay

0m   100m

Camps Bay's war memorial commemorates local men who lost their lives during the two World Wars.

Farquhar, a strong-minded man who was determined to market Camps Bay as a holiday resort as well as a desirable place to live. The planting of palm trees along the beach front was one of Farquhar's ideas. A second tramline climbed over the Kloof Nek pass to the west of Table Mountain, which was a major engineering feat. It opened a year later.

Continue along Victoria Road to reach the **Theatre on the Bay** ❸ in Link Street. Part of the theatre incorporates walls that once housed the engine room of a power station. The Camps Bay syndicate had built this to provide electricity for the tramway. At one stage, the theatre was the Alvin Cinema, then the Phoenix Theatre, used by a local amateur dramatic group, until it was damaged by fire and relaunched as the Theatre on the Bay by theatre impresario Pieter Toerien.

As part of the plan to entice visitors to the seaside by showing them how close Camps Bay was to the city, the syndicate also built a covered swimming pool with warm water heated by the power station. Opposite and behind the police station, a portion of these **old swimming baths** ❹ can be seen.

This plaque pays tribute to Philly, a horse that became a local institution.

On the corner of Victoria and Link roads is a **war memorial** ❺ to the men of the suburb who lost their lives in World Wars I and II. Return to the pedestrian crossing over Camps Bay Drive and walk up the Drive. To the side of the car park is the library. On the stairway there is a **plaque** ❻ commemorating Philly, with the inscription '1932–1967 Freedom of Camps Bay'. This horse, although stabled in the village, seemed to spend most of his time wandering around the soccer field and beach front. In his later years, he had a donkey as a companion. Philly was a local institution and residents delighted in feeding him titbits. On the right is the primary school, the stone-clad portion dating from 1914.

A little further on, on the left, is the **Rotunda** ❼, now part of the Bay Hotel. This popular establishment, which served as an entertainment hall hosting dances, music-hall acts, boxing matches as well as roller-skating contests, was opened on 19 May 1904 as yet another attraction provided by Cape Marine Suburbs Limited. The company also laid out a bowling green and a golf course. The latter, however, was unsuccessful and closed.

Going strong since 1904 is the former entertainment hall, the Rotunda.

By 1922 the company had not sold as many building plots as hoped. The novelty of tram rides had waned and the arrival of omnibuses, which could travel on any route and were more cost-effective, reduced the tram company's profitability. On 16 February 1930, the last tram left Camps Bay. The tramway operation became insolvent and closed.

In 1936 Isidore Cohen bought the shares of both the Camps Bay Tramways Company and Cape Marine Suburbs, and thereby acquired all the land between the beach and the Pipe Track, excluding the few existing private properties. Camps Bay slowly developed into a residential suburb after World War II, and is now a sought-after, popular neighbourhood.

From the Rotunda return to the starting point.

THE ROUNDHOUSE

The Roundhouse ❽, an unusual building down towards the Glen in Camps Bay, was probably built on the foundation of a round fortification placed here by the Dutch in the 1600s. The land was granted to Jan Horak in 1814, who built a mainly wooden construction that was used as a shooting box by Lord Charles Somerset, governor of the Cape Colony from 1814 to 1826. Somerset had a summer residence in Camps Bay and shot buck, a lion and a leopard in what was then a wild, remote area. One of Somerset's friends and a likely visitor to the shooting box was Dr James Barry, the assistant surgeon at the Cape, known for his shrill voice and argumentative temper. Barry later became a surgeon major and finally inspector general of the British Army Medical Corps. When he died in London in 1865, it was discovered that he was a woman.

The Roundhouse, which has survived two fires, has been extensively altered over the years and has operated as a hotel and restaurant. It has recently been restored and since 2008 has been an award-winning restaurant with magnificent views.

DISTANCE
6 km

TERRAIN
Slight slopes

EFFORT
Easy

USEFUL INFORMATION

Heritage Museum
admission charge;
discount for children
021 786 2302

Simon's Town Museum
donation
021 786 3046

Simon's Town Tourism
021 786 5880

South African Naval Museum
free admission;
admission to the Martello
tower can be arranged here
021 787 4635
www.navy.mil.za

Warrior Toy Museum
admission charge
021 786 1395

For information on all Simon's Town museums
www.simonstown.org

REFRESHMENTS

■ Good choice of restaurants and coffee shops
■ Salty Sea Dog for good fish and chips, 6 Wharf Street (no bookings)

Simon's Town Harbour

Simon's Town

This naval town on the False Bay coast has plenty to explore, with alleys and passageways branching off the main street.

The town and harbour are named after Governor Simon van der Stel, who visited this area in 1687. In 1742, after the loss of ships in Table Bay during north-westerly winter gales, the VOC arranged for its ships to use Simon's Bay from 15 May to 15 August each year. As a result, Dutch East India Company buildings and stores were erected and a small fishing village developed. After the second British occupation of the Cape in 1806, Simon's Town grew in importance, and in 1814 it became the British naval base, which necessitated housing, storage and provisions for the navy.

The local Historical Society has done a great job over the past 50 years or so in erecting information plaques and issuing pamphlets on the local history of Simon's Town. Many buildings on St George's Street have a historical background, so only the ones that are most important and interesting are mentioned. The town also has five museums and several other tourist attractions.

Although this is a long walk, there are lots of places for refreshments along the way.

THE WALK

Start at the **railway station** ❶ at the north end of town. It was built in 1890 and has an attractive double-storey station house. The railway line opened in December 1890 to great fanfare, with the then prime minister of the Cape Colony, Cecil John Rhodes, giving a speech at the opening ceremony.

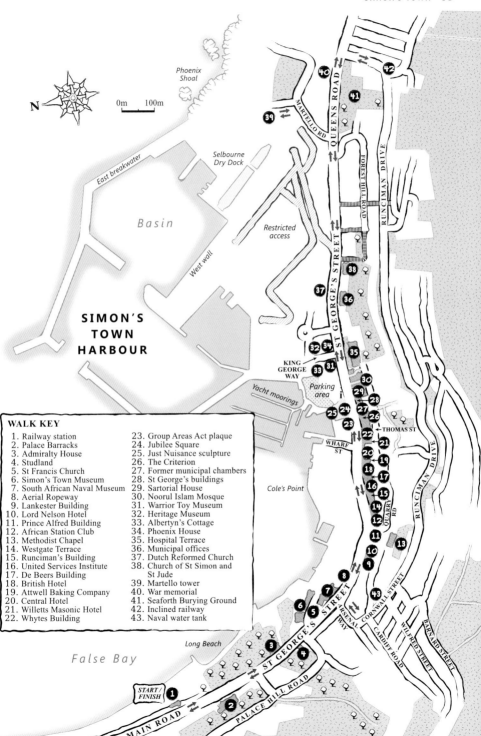

Phoenix Shoal

N 0m 100m

Selbourne Dry Dock

East breakwater

Basin

West wall

Restricted access

SIMON'S TOWN HARBOUR

KING GEORGE WAY

Yacht moorings

Parking area

Cole's Point

WHARF ST

THOMAS ST

WALK KEY

1. Railway station
2. Palace Barracks
3. Admiralty House
4. Studland
5. St Francis Church
6. Simon's Town Museum
7. South African Naval Museum
8. Aerial Ropeway
9. Lankester Building
10. Lord Nelson Hotel
11. Prince Alfred Building
12. African Station Club
13. Methodist Chapel
14. Westgate Terrace
15. Runciman's Building
16. United Services Institute
17. De Beers Building
18. British Hotel
19. Attwell Baking Company
20. Central Hotel
21. Willetts Masonic Hotel
22. Whytes Building
23. Group Areas Act plaque
24. Jubilee Square
25. Just Nuisance sculpture
26. The Criterion
27. Former municipal chambers
28. St George's buildings
29. Sartorial House
30. Noorul Islam Mosque
31. Warrior Toy Museum
32. Heritage Museum
33. Albertyn's Cottage
34. Phoenix House
35. Hospital Terrace
36. Municipal offices
37. Dutch Reformed Church
38. Church of St Simon and St Jude
39. Martello tower
40. War memorial
41. Seaforth Burying Ground
42. Inclined railway
43. Naval water tank

Long Beach

False Bay

START / FINISH

MAIN ROAD

PALACE HILL ROAD

ST GEORGE'S STREET

QUEENS ROAD

MARTELLO RD

FOREST HILL ROAD

RUNCIMAN DRIVE

QUARRY RD

ARSENAL WAY

CORNWALL STREET

CARDIFF ROAD

WILFRED STREET

BARNARD STREET

The old Admiralty House, now the residence of the chief of the South African Navy

Opposite is the **Palace Barracks** ❷, restored in 2006 and used for naval purposes. This was originally a private house, then it became a hotel, and was later used as a military mess before being turned into a hospital in 1900 for Boer prisoners. Mary Kingsley, a British scientist, writer and explorer (niece of writer Charles Kingsley), volunteered to work in the Cape in 1900 to nurse Boer War prisoners. She worked in horrific conditions and caught typhoid; she died shortly afterwards in Simon's Town, aged 37. She was given a naval burial at sea.

Beyond the station is the wall of **Admiralty House** ❸, over which it is possible to glimpse the gardens. The Royal Navy purchased a house here in 1814, and after major renovations it became the official home of the commander-in-chief of the Royal Navy Cape Squadron in 1853. Many social functions were held here. It is now the residence of the chief of the South African Navy.

Studland ❹, across St George's Street, dates from 1797, when it was a tavern. A brewery was added in 1874 and it has been converted to a private residence.

As you head into town, on the left is the Anglican **Church of St Francis** ❺. This has changed considerably from the building erected in 1837 with funds collected by the Cape governor's wife, Lady Frances Cole. Down Court Road the building known as The Residency is now the **Simon's Town Museum** **6**. Built in 1777 as the winter residence for the governor of the Cape, it served a number of purposes. It has been used as a naval hospital, customs house, port captain's office, post office, school, gaol and a magistrates' court. Today it has a good selection of exhibits, including memorabilia about the famous Great Dane, Able Seaman Just Nuisance.

JUST NUISANCE – THE SAILORS' DOG

The only dog to have the honour of being made an able seaman in the Royal Navy was a thoroughbred Great Dane born on 1 April 1937. His owner, Benjamin Chaney, was appointed manager of the United Services Institute in Simon's Town, which catered for the welfare and comfort of servicemen and -women stationed at the naval base or on Royal Navy ships docked in Simon's Town Harbour. Most of the patrons at the institute were naval ratings, and Just Nuisance soon befriended the bell-bottomed 'Jack Tars'. He followed them on board ship and accompanied them on train journeys to Cape Town. After they had visited the pubs of the city, the dog would guide and protect them on the journey back to Simon's Town. As he never had a ticket, the South African Railways complained about the dog – and he earned his name, Nuisance. The railways threatened to have him put down, which caused a huge outcry in the naval town, where he had become well known. The commander-in-chief officially enlisted him in the Royal Navy. He was then given the name Able Seaman Just Nuisance.

He was given a naval cap, a bunk in the barracks at Froggy Pond and, most importantly, a rail pass. He attended fund-raising and war-charity functions on a lead with a sailor handler. He fathered a litter of puppies, which were auctioned for war charities.

Around 1943 he started to visit Wingfield, a Royal Navy air station near Goodwood, where he was, on at least two occasions, taken on flights on an Albacore reconnaissance aircraft until a senior officer put an end to this.

He was adored by the young ratings, who enjoyed his company. He was injured by a car and admitted to the Navy Hospital. He died on 1 April 1944, seven years to the day after his birth. He was wrapped in a white ensign and, to the sound of the 'Last Post', buried at Klaver Camp above Simon's Town, where his grave can be visited. Nearby is a memorial to seamen who died in World War I.

Directions: To visit the grave of Just Nuisance, take the main road out of Simon's Town towards Fish Hoek. Turn left onto the Red Hill Road, and on the plateau on the left take the road to the old South African Navy Signal Station (the former Naval Sanatorium), open from 9 a.m. to 3 p.m. daily. The gatekeeper will give further directions.

ERHARDT THIEL/IOA

The South African Naval Museum has a collection of intriguing naval-history memorabilia.

Back on St George's Street, on the left is the **South African Naval Museum ❼**, which has a fascinating naval-history collection that includes models, paintings, pictures, guns, torpedoes, rafts, boats, depth charges and even a helicopter.

Next door is a metal pylon that was part of the **Aerial Ropeway ❽**, which ran from the dockyard up to the sanatorium on Red Hill. It operated from 1904 to 1927, transporting sailors and stores up the hill. Keep to the left-hand pavement, as there are plaques on the wall that provide historical background.

No. 54 St George's Street (**Lankester Building**) ❾ was built in 1902. The architect, John Parker of the firm Parker & Forsyth, at one stage lived in Simon's Town and a number of the Victorian buildings are his design.

Next door, the **Lord Nelson Hotel ❿** was a lodging house in 1829. Ohlsson's Brewery bought it in 1887 and it was remodelled in 1929 by Parker & Forsyth, and the name changed to the Lord Nelson. Nelson's ship was anchored in Simon's Bay when the future admiral was serving as a young midshipman, but it is unclear if he actually came ashore.

No. 62 St George's was another hotel, the **Prince Alfred ⓫**, also owned by Ohlsson's Brewery and named after Queen Victoria's son, who visited Simon's Town in 1860.

On the corner of Quarry Road is another naval building. The old **African Station Club** ⑫, built in 1873 from locally quarried stone, was a facility for Royal Navy sailors. Look up Quarry Road at the **Methodist Chapel** ⑬, built in 1828 as the Wesleyan Chapel. This is the oldest church in the town and the oldest church of its denomination in South Africa.

In St George's Street, at Nos 76–78, is **Westgate Terrace** ⑭, a pair of double-storey buildings acquired by the Royal Navy for various purposes. The buildings later housed the Royal Navy Club, and are now used by the South African Navy.

No. 82, known as **Runciman's Building** ⑮, was built in 1785. In 1899 John Parker remodelled the front in the Victorian style. The building was named after William Runciman, a local businessman and mayor of Simon's Town on five occasions.

No. 84, the old **United Services Institute** ⑯, was built in 1905. It was well known in World War II as the first home of Just Nuisance (see page 95). On the right, the window with an anchor emblem was the doorway into the building and the place where the dog liked to nap.

Located at No. 88, the **De Beers Building** ⑰ was designed by Sir Herbert Baker for the De Beers Company. It was later converted into a cold-storage facility to provide frozen meat for the Royal Navy. It was taken over in 1921 by Standard Bank, and since 1973 has functioned as a restaurant.

Right next door is the **British Hotel** ⑱. Designed by John Parker, it has been a feature of the main street for many years. Victorian explorer and writer Mary Kingsley stayed there while nursing Boer prisoners during the Anglo-Boer War. After falling into disuse, the hotel was restored in 1991.

The former doorway to the United Services Institute, where Just Nuisance used to sleep, has been replaced by a window (above). The British Hotel was restored in 1991 (below).

No. 94 St George's Street was home to the Attwell Baking Company (above). A plaque in Jubilee Square honours the memory of those affected by forced removals (below).

No. 94 was remodelled in 1897 by John Parker to provide premises for the **Attwell Baking Company** ⑲, hence the letters 'ABC' on the gable. Attwell's had a contract with the Royal Navy to provide bread. The bakery closed in 1929. Next door, the former **Central Hotel** ⑳ was operated by Ohlsson's Brewery from 1898. The hotel closed its doors in 1966.

At one stage during the British Navy's tenure, Simon's Town had six hotels, all with bars. No. 108 was one of them. Known as **Willetts Masonic Hotel** ㉑, it was remodelled by John Parker in 1898 for Ohlsson's Brewery.

No. 110 St George's Street, **Whytes Building** ㉒, started off as a bakery in 1852 and was rebuilt by John Parker in 1910, which explains the appearance of different dates on the gables.

Across the road, on the sidewalk in front of Jubilee Square, is a **plaque** ㉓ explaining how a section of Simon's Town's population was removed under the terms of the Group Areas Act. The 1960 census gives a population breakdown of 3 462 whites, 3 579 coloured people, 115 Indians and about 1 500 black people. On 1 September 1967, Simon's Town was proclaimed a white group area and the rest of the population was forced to move. The effect on business was marked, and added to the problem was the fact that the government kept more than 100 houses empty as an option for housing the navy.

In **Jubilee Square** ㉔ is the much-visited sculpture of Simon's Town's famous dog, **Just Nuisance** ㉕, by Jean Doyle. Nearby is the Queen Victoria Diamond Jubilee Fountain of 1899, which was moved from St George's Street, the main road. Jubilee Square was named in 1935 to commemorate the silver jubilee of King George V. Opposite, in St George's Street, is the

The **Criterion** 🕮, where the Criterion Cinema opened in 1926. The cinema was very popular with Royal Navy ratings and the local coloured community. The Royal Navy left Simon's Town in 1957 and the forced removals began in 1967, resulting in the cinema going out of business.

Simon's Town's famous dog, Just Nuisance, sculpted by Jean Doyle

The next building on St George's Street, with the motif STM (Simon's Town Municipality), served as the **municipal chambers** 🕮 between 1913 and 1945.

St George's buildings 🕮 were also remodelled by architect John Parker and converted into a hotel around 1910. Ohlsson's Brewery owned it when it closed in 1966. This was the year the star-grading policy was introduced for licensed hotels, and those that could not afford the facilities demanded by the Hotel Board were forced to close.

Sartorial House 🕮 housed the naval tailors and outfitters, A.T. Manuel and Son, for 54 years.

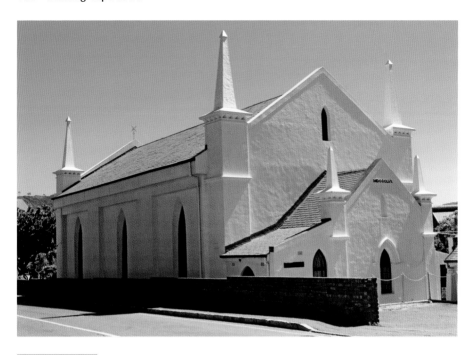

The Simon's Town Dutch Reformed Church was built in 1856.

At the top of Alfred Lane is the **Noorul Islam Mosque** ㉚. This used to be a private house where, from 1888, prayers were held. It was rebuilt in 1926.

On the shore side of St George's Street is the **Warrior Toy Museum** ㉛, which houses a great collection of toys and dolls from years past. The display, which includes working exhibits, will fascinate young and old alike.

Walk down King George Way; on the right is the **Heritage Museum** ㉜ in Amlay House. The museum was started by the Noorul Islam Historical Society to serve as a reminder of the vibrant community that lived in Simon's Town before the apartheid-era forced removals.

Adjacent to the parking area is **Albertyn's Cottage** ㉝. The stables are now used as a foundry. The cottage was built circa 1800 as a store. It has been used for a number of purposes and it is named after Nicholas Albertyn, who lived there in the early 1800s.

Back up the road, look out for **Phoenix House** ㉞ on the left corner. Built in 1860 as a single-storey customs house, it became the Salvation Army Hall and was converted to a double-storey building, the Phoenix Masonic Lodge. It is named after the *Phoenix*, a British ship that sank off Seaforth Beach in 1829.

Across the road, behind the stone wall, is **Hospital Terrace** , built in 1813 by the Royal Navy as a hospital and staff quarters. It closed in 1904 and is now used by the South African Navy.

The **municipal offices** 🠲 and the local library are housed in the former Simon's Town Secondary School, a large and attractive building designed by John Parker in 1896.

On the other side of the road is the **Dutch Reformed Church** 🠲, built in 1856 with a thatched roof. Next to the church is the Victorian-style rectory. It was here that Reverend M.L. de Villiers composed the music in 1921 for South Africa's former national anthem, 'Die Stem van Suid-Afrika'. The words were written by the poet C.J. Langenhoven.

Across the road is the **Church of St Simon and St Jude** 🠲, a handsome Roman Catholic church built in 1885 with local stone.

The Roman Catholic Church of St Simon and St Jude was built in 1885 (above). Nearby is a memorial to Boer prisoners of war (left).

The road to the **Martello tower** 🠲 skirts the dockyard wall. The tower, built in 1796, is possibly the first building constructed by the British in South Africa. It is based on a circular defensive tower in Corsica, which caused the British fleet to withdraw a planned attack there during the Napoleonic Wars.

Back on the main road, on the left is a **war memorial** 🠲 and opposite is the old **Seaforth Burying Ground** 🠲. Dating from 1813, the cemetery contains a number of interesting graves, including an Anglo-Boer War memorial to the Boer prisoners of war who died in the prison camp nearby.

Then, up Runciman Drive is a plaque denoting the site of the **inclined railway** 🠲, which was designed to transport stone from the nearby quarry for building the eastern dockyard.

On the way back, a short distance up Arsenal Way, is the old naval stone **water tank** 🠲 used to collect water for Royal Navy ships.

Jager's Walk

Sea gulls are among
the many seabirds
encountered along the
False Bay coastline.
ALBERT FRONEMAN/IOA

Fish Hoek: Jager's Walk

The False Bay town of Fish Hoek has a lovely beach and an
undulating walkway along the rocks. The walkway was the
initiative of Herman Scott Jager, a local and chairman
of the village management board. Jager persuaded
the board to apply for funding for a walkway in 1931,
to provide access to rock pools and create a safe place
for sea fishing. Subsequent funding extended the route
to Sunny Cove Station. In 1940 Fish Hoek became a
municipality and Jager the first mayor of the town.

Southern Right Whales calve in the waters of False Bay between August and November.

PETER & BEVERLY PICKFORD/IOA

THE WALK

Today the path, also known locally as the 'catwalk', is reached by a bridge over the railway line at **Sunny Cove Station ❶**.

There is a **whale-watching point ❷** and the path skirts the rocks. There are steps down to a natural **rock pool ❸** suitable for swimming. Several benches line the route, many sponsored by local residents and businesses. Three subways provide access to Main Road.

The walk ends at **Fish Hoek Beach ❹**, where there is an eatery and takeaway facilities.

There is limited street parking, but paid parking is available near Fish Hoek Beach.

FISH HOEK VALLEY MUSEUM

Situated in a house next to the Civic Centre, the Fish Hoek Valley Museum ❺ has a diorama and display on Peers Cave, where the skull of the 15 000-year-old 'Fish Hoek Man' was discovered by Victor Peers and his son Bertie in 1927.

Other rooms have photographs and items of local interest. It is staffed by helpful volunteers. Donations are appreciated.

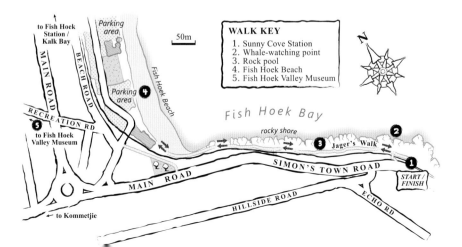

WALK KEY
1. Sunny Cove Station
2. Whale-watching point
3. Rock pool
4. Fish Hoek Beach
5. Fish Hoek Valley Museum

SHAEN ADEY/IOA

Kalk Bay

Kalk Bay

Kalk Bay is a fishing village on the False Bay coastline that is packed with character and charm. In addition, it is one of the few places on the peninsula where you can buy fish on the quayside, fresh from the boats working out of the harbour.

A stroll along Main Road affords the opportunity to look at a variety of clothing shops and to snoop around in the second-hand shops for collectibles. Between August and early November, Southern Right Whales, which come into False Bay at that time to calve, are frequently spotted.

The name of the village derives from lime, or *kalk*, produced by burning shells in kilns, an industry here from the late 1600s to the mid-1850s.

In the eighteenth century, the 25-mile road journey from Cape Town to Simon's Town entailed the hazards of quicksands and difficult terrain beyond Kalk Bay. The Dutch often had to unload their goods into boats here and ship them to their end destination. The empty carts, which parked at the Outspan in Kalk Bay, would return to Cape Town laden with lime from the kilns and fish from the harbour.

This gentle walk follows Main Road and then diverts to the harbour and up to the fishermen's cottages.

Kalk Bay Harbour is home to a multitude of Cape fur seals.
PETER & BEVERLY PICKFORD/IOA

THE WALK

The walk starts at **Kalk Bay Station ❶** – note the two chimneys still on the building. The railway reached Kalk Bay in May 1883. The Cape Government Railway Company acquired a house, which it then had converted into a railway station. From the Kalk Bay Station, turn right onto the pavement on the seaward side. Steep steps down to the subway lead to the Brass Bell restaurant.

Keep to the pavement. The first building is the **old post office ❷**, built in 1935. On the wall is an attractive mural designed by a local ceramic artist, dated 1936. Similar murals can be found in the old Muizenberg and St James post offices (see page 112). Next to the post office is a delightful garden tended by local residents.

It was customary for the railways to provide accommodation for their station masters. The former **railway house ❸** has been converted into a second-hand shop.

A little further on, past an indigenous garden, is the **Dale Brook tidal pool ❹**, complete with toilets and changing rooms. A combination of private and municipal funding in 1906 led to a sea wall being erected; by 1914 the pool was completed.

Opposite Jacobs Ladder, the steps that run up to Boyes Drive, is **Danger Beach ❺**, where whaling used to take place. Whaling was the third most profitable industry in the Cape Colony after agriculture and winemaking in the early nineteenth century. **Villa Capri ❻** was the site of the old whaling station and the carcasses were cut up on Danger Beach. **No. 82 Main Road ❼** was originally a whaler's cottage. Cross Main Road and go back the way you came, on the opposite side of the road.

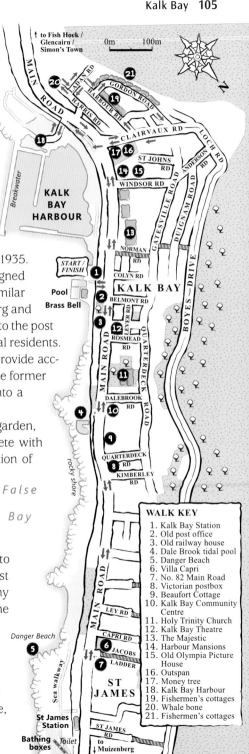

WALK KEY
1. Kalk Bay Station
2. Old post office
3. Old railway house
4. Dale Brook tidal pool
5. Danger Beach
6. Villa Capri
7. No. 82 Main Road
8. Victorian postbox
9. Beaufort Cottage
10. Kalk Bay Community Centre
11. Holy Trinity Church
12. Kalk Bay Theatre
13. The Majestic
14. Harbour Mansions
15. Old Olympia Picture House
16. Outspan
17. Money tree
18. Kalk Bay Harbour
19. Fishermen's cottages
20. Whale bone
21. Fishermen's cottages

STONEWORK

As you walk around Kalk Bay, you will notice a number of properties constructed using local stone from the mountain. There were several quarries on Kalk Bay Mountain, and during the late nineteenth century, when a number of grand seaside houses were built, stonemasons were hired from Britain, who imparted their skills to the local artisans.

In the wall of the house next to Quarterdeck Road is an **old postbox** ❽ with the insignia V.R., from Queen Victoria's reign. **Beaufort Cottage** ❾, at No. 12 Main Road, was the holiday home of Sir John Molteno, first prime minister of the Cape Colony. You will pass a number of large homes facing the sea, some of which have become guesthouses. The extension of the railway line made this area popular, and these houses were built in the late 1800s or early 1900s as seaside homes for Cape Town's gentry.

The **Kalk Bay Community Centre** ❿, with the inscription on the facade 'KBMM 1905', was built as a sewerage pump station for the Kalk Bay/Muizenberg Municipality, which existed from 1895 to 1913, when it became part of the Cape Town Municipality. During World War II, the building was acquired by the Kalk Bay branch of the South African Women's Auxiliary Services for use as a canteen and entertainment facility for soldiers and navy personnel passing through the Cape. It was later used as a library; it has now been converted for community use. The lamp posts at the entrance bear the crest of the old Kalk Bay Municipality and were manufactured in London circa 1900.

Situated in a pretty garden, the **Holy Trinity Church** ⓫, constructed from stone hewn from a quarry on Kalk Bay Mountain, was completed in 1874. It was designed by London architect Henry Woodyer and is modelled on a church in Bristol. The main finance for the church was provided by the Humphrey sisters, who came from that town. The lychgate at the churchyard entrance is said to be the oldest in South Africa.

The lychgate at the Holy Trinity Church

In the next block, the **Kalk Bay Theatre** ⓬ was originally a Dutch Reformed Church. Its consecration service, on 26 April 1878, was attended by more than 600 people. The church closed in January 1950 and has subsequently been used for a number of commercial purposes. In 2001 it became a theatre. Note the blue-and-white mural of tiles on the front wall sponsored by the Kalk Bay Historical Society.

Carry on past the shops to **The Majestic** ⓭, a handsomely renovated apartment complex. Originally, the Masonic Hotel stood on this site. In 1913 Ohlsson's Brewery decided to demolish the hotel and replace it with a single-storey building known today as the

Local stone was quarried to build the Holy Trinity Church.

Kalk Bay
Harbour with
the fishermen's
cottages in the
background

Annex, which is used as a restaurant. The stone building in front used to be a public bar and off-sales bottle store, and was locally known as the Klipkantien (Stone Canteen). The three-storey Majestic Hotel was designed in 1916 by the architect John Parker. The Union-Castle Line bought the hotel in 1929 and after major renovations and additions ran it as a sister hotel to the Mount Nelson. It advertised the hotel as the 'pride of False Bay', offering its passengers from England accommodation on the coast with the attraction of sea bathing. In 1939 the company sold the hotel, after which it was privately owned until 1970, when it became an old-persons' home and fell into a state of disrepair. The building on the Windsor Road side of the site was the New King's Hotel. Designed by W.H. Grant, the interior of the hotel boasted a number of art deco features. It was run by South African Breweries but closed in 1970, after which it, too, served as an old-age home. The two buildings were finally incorporated into the redevelopment of The Majestic.

The next building on Main Road is **Harbour Mansions ⑭**, erected as a boarding house in 1906. Next door, in Windsor Road, is the old **Olympia Picture House ⑮**, Kalk Bay's first cinema. The name later changed to The Olympia. The balcony seating was reserved for 'non-white' patrons. During intervals audiences found the bars of the New King's Hotel, just across the road, an added attraction. The cinema closed after a fire in 1968. The premises are now used as a bakery. From the bakery's retail shop, in St Johns Road next to the parking area on the Outspan, you can sometimes get a view of the inside of the building, complete with the original balcony.

The **Outspan ⑯** was an open area used by ox wagons and horses and carts. There is a tree on the corner that locals call the **money tree ⑰** because in the 1850s and later, it was where the fishing-boat skippers paid their crews. Cross the road at the pedestrian traffic lights and head for the harbour. You will see the railway viaduct built out of mountain stone. A small piece of sandy beach denotes where Fishery Beach was. In the early 1850s, there were about 50 fishing boats working from this beach.

In the **harbour** ⓲, work on constructing the breakwater began in 1913; it remains in use today. It is possible to walk along it, but caution should be exercised during heavy seas, as people have been washed into the sea. It is well worth a visit to the fish quay, particularly if a catch is being brought in. There are a number of eating options in the harbour area, from takeaways to fine dining.

When you come out of the harbour, cross Main Road and walk up Clairvaux Road, past the wall built from local stone, to Harbour Road, and turn left. A short way along is the first group of **fishermen's cottages** ⓳. These were built by the City Council in 1941. They have a living room, two bedrooms, kitchen, bathroom and toilet.

Turn left into Ladan Road and right into Harris Road. Next to the gate at the end of the road is a dry white stump. This is a **whale bone** ⓴ that is more than 150 years old, used as a boundary marker (whale bones were also used as fencing). Retrace your steps and go along Gordon Road, where the final group of 34 **fishermen's cottages** ㉑ was completed in 1947. The playground was added by the municipality; the St James Mission School was built by the Roman Catholic Church. An interesting feature of the houses is the lanterns over the entrances with the numbers cut out of the lantern covers. The tenants survived the implementation of the Group Areas Act and received a dispensation from being forcibly removed. In later years, the cottages were sold to their tenants under a sectional-title scheme.

Turn back down Clairvaux Road to Main Road and the starting point. Incidentally, Boyes Drive, at the top of Clairvaux Road, is named after George Boyes, chief magistrate of Simon's Town between 1904 and 1916. It was built by convict labour.

WHALING

Southern Right Whales return annually to calve in False Bay – from August to early November. The first shore-based whaling operations started near Simon's Town in the early nineteenth century. Because of complaints from the navy about the smell, these operations moved along the coast to St James. After the arrival of the railway line in 1883 and the development of seaside homes, complaints from residents forced the industry to move to Muizenberg, east of Zandvlei, until the early twentieth century.

Whale bones were used as fencing and to mark property boundaries.

USEFUL INFORMATION

Battlements and Posthuys
open by appointment;
donation box
021 788 5951

Casa Labia
021 788 6068
info@casalabia.co.za

Muizenberg Tourism
021 787 9140

Rhodes Cottage Museum
donation box
021 788 7673

REFRESHMENTS

Cafés along Main Road in St James and Muizenberg and opposite Surfers' Corner

Bathing boxes, Muizenberg Beach

Muizenberg & St James

The name of the seaside suburb of Muizenberg, is thought to come from Wynard Willem Muijs, a VOC official in 1743 who resided at Steenberghoek (near present-day Zandvlei). Another theory is that there is a rock on Muizenberg Mountain that looks like a mouse if viewed from a certain angle.

This leisurely walk, skirting False Bay's coastline between Muizenberg and St James, combines a sea walkway and the grand old houses of Millionaires' Row.

It is wise to undertake this walk at low tide, and best to have a companion, as the walkway is isolated in places.

THE WALK

Start at the traffic circle at Surfers' Corner near Muizenberg Beach and pick up the walkway near Muizenberg railway station. The walkway runs along the rocks and follows the coastline.

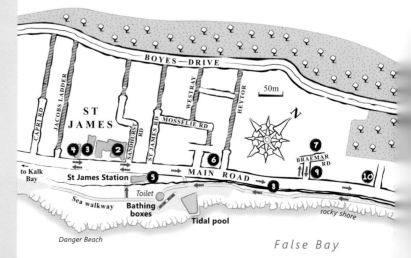

The first section of the walkway, which ran as far as Bailey's Cottage, was created by the City Council, with generous financial assistance from a local businessman and resident, Mendel Kaplan. The walkway was opened on 22 December 1987 by the mayor of Cape Town. A couple of years later, with backing from the same benefactor, the amenity was extended to St James. It offers stunning views over False Bay and a refreshing breath of sea air. A few commemorative benches are positioned along the way. Views across the railway line highlight the different architectural styles of buildings above Main Road.

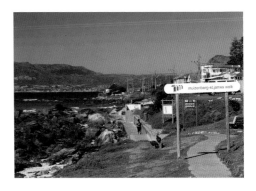

The start of the sea walkway, which follows the railway line from Muizenberg to St James

Bailey's Cottage ❶, on the sea side of the walkway, was built in 1909 and designed by architects Baker & Massey. Further on, the tidal pool at St James has brightly coloured beach huts and a large grassed area with a toilet block. The path continues to the sandy Danger Beach.

Use the subway at St James Station and the steps to reach Main Road. You can return along the walkway to the starting point, but there is a lot to see on Main Road. Turn left and keep to the Main Road pavement. The first building is the **St James Retirement Centre ❷** on the opposite side of the road. At the middle of this rambling complex is an old house built in 1897

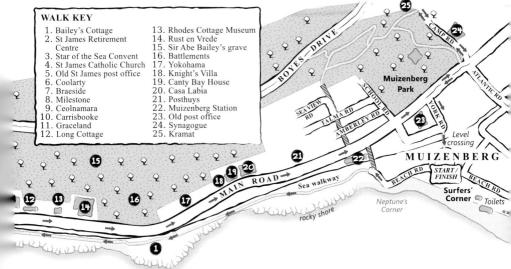

WALK KEY

1. Bailey's Cottage
2. St James Retirement Centre
3. Star of the Sea Convent
4. St James Catholic Church
5. Old St James post office
6. Coolarty
7. Braeside
8. Milestone
9. Ceolnamara
10. Carrisbooke
11. Graceland
12. Long Cottage
13. Rhodes Cottage Museum
14. Rust en Vrede
15. Sir Abe Bailey's grave
16. Battlements
17. Yokohama
18. Knight's Villa
19. Canty Bay House
20. Casa Labia
21. Posthuys
22. Muizenberg Station
23. Old post office
24. Synagogue
25. Kramat

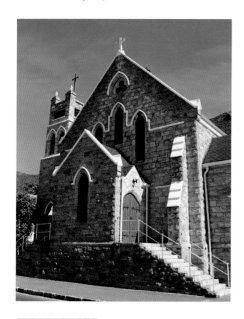

St James Catholic Church

Mural of Simon van der Stel on the exterior wall of the old post office building

for J.W. Attwell of Attwell's Bakery Company, called La Rivage. This was extended over the years and became the St James Hotel in 1903, popular until 1990, when it closed.

Next door, the attractive **Star of the Sea Convent ❸**, a double-storey stone building, was built in 1906 as a seaside home for nuns recovering from illness. It was designed by Father John Duignam. It has been a Roman Catholic school since 1914. Next up is **St James Catholic Church ❹**. Father Duignam was instrumental in designing and building the church, using stone from the Kalk Bay mountains. The original chapel was on land below Main Road and had to be demolished to make way for the railway in 1882. The chapel catered for a group of Filipino fishermen who had been shipwrecked and had settled in Kalk Bay. For the new church, Father Duignam used some of his Filipino congregants, as well as Italian stonemasons working on the Selbourne Dockyard at Simon's Town, as helpers. St James takes its name from this church. Turn around here and head back towards Muizenberg along the Main Road.

The St James railway station was built in 1928, as was the old **post office ❺**, which closed in 1995. Note the tile mosaics.

VAN DER STEL EXPLORES THE PENINSULAR FROM ST JAMES IN 1693

VAN ST JAMES AF VERKEN VAN DER STEL IN 1695 DIE SKIEREILAND

One depicts Simon Van der Stel exploring St James and the other commemorates the naming of St James.

Main Road follows the path that ox wagons used during the VOC period to reach Simon's Town. It wasn't until the second British occupation and the decision to establish Simon's Town as the naval base that the road was improved. Until then, flooding, quicksands, marshy ground and drifting sand dunes were regular hazards. The British built a military hard road, constructed and maintained by convict labour. A toll system was introduced. A daily horse-drawn post cart operated between Cape Town and Simon's Town in 1850, as well as stage coaches and horse-drawn omnibuses. Farmer Peck's Inn in Muizenberg was a popular stopping place for refreshment. The railway line reached Muizenberg in 1882, and Simon's Town in 1890. This, and the arrival of the first cars a few years later, led to the development of large seaside houses. This section onwards is known as Millionaires' Row. Among these homes are **Coolarty** ❻ (No. 42), built in 1911, and **Braeside** ❼ (Braemar Road, 1914), which belonged to the Wiley family for many years. Note the slate **milestone** ❽ on the shore-side pavement opposite No. 32. **Ceolnamara** ❾ (20 Main Road) was designed by Baker & Massey with traditional twin gables. **Carrisbooke** ❿ is a symmetrical Victorian residence dating from 1879. Inside the Muizenberg boundary, No. 252, now named **Graceland** ⓫ (originally Watergate), was built for the Garlick family in the 1920s and designed by architect W.H. Grant.

Long Cottage ⓬ is the most impressive of the thatched cottages along this stretch of the road. It was used by Governor Sir Henry Barkly in 1872 as a seaside home. Further along, **Rhodes Cottage** ⓭, built in the 1880s, was bought by Cecil John Rhodes in 1899 to use

This milestone in St James (XVI) is one of eight remaining slate milestones that were erected in 1830 between the Old Town House on Greenmarket Square in central Cape Town and Simon's Town.

Canty Bay House (above); Knight's Villa (below)

as a summer retreat. Rhodes died here on 26 March 1902. It is now a museum run on a voluntary basis by members of the Muizenberg Historical Conservation Society.

Rust en Vrede ⓮ considered by many to be one of Herbert Baker's best works. The land belonged to Rhodes, and Baker was planning a house for him. After Rhodes's death, Sir Abe Bailey purchased the land, and the house was built in 1905. On the hill behind the house, **Sir Abe Bailey's grave ⓯** can be seen from Boyes Drive and the battlement site.

The Battle of Muizenberg (7 August 1795) is commemorated at an open-air museum, where the **battlements ⓰** can be visited by appointment. Four British warships opened fire on the Dutch forces, who moved off to near where Retreat is today.

No. 210, **Yokohama ⓱**, is a papier mâché Japanese-style house constructed circa 1906. **Knight's Villa ⓲**, originally called Stonehouse, was designed in 1899 by the architect George Ransome for a certain Mr Knight in the style of a Venetian palazzo. **Canty Bay House ⓳**, at

No. 196 Main Road, partly dates from 1899. The anchor at the front of the house seems to represent a connection with a previous owner, Admiral H.H. Biermann, a former chief of the South African Navy. **Casa Labia** ⓴, originally known as the Fort, is now a family-run museum, art gallery and restaurant. The architect, F.M. Glennie, designed it for Count Labia in 1929. Casa Labia is well worth a visit. No. 186 is the former Carnegie Library; it was opened by colonial secretary N.F. de Waal in April 1910. It was built with funds provided by the Carnegie Trust to introduce libraries into English-speaking countries. This building and the old post office next door (circa 1911) housed the South African Police Museum, which is now closed. When the post office moved, the building became the police station, which then subsequently moved to its present site.

A little further on is the **Posthuys** ㉑; there is some contention about its exact date – it certainly was in operation around 1730/1740. It was used for a number of purposes, serving as a storeroom and an ale and eating house. It was restored by the Anglo American Corporation in 1982/3 to its original state. It is now a museum and is open by appointment.

Casa Labia, now an art gallery, is one of the most noteworthy buildings on Muizenberg's Millionaires' Row.

Ceramic-tile mural outside the old post office (above); railway station clock tower (below)

Across the road is the new **Muizenberg Station ㉒**, built in 1913. This is the second station to have been constructed on this site. Designed by J.C. Tully and built by W. Delbridge & Co., it is a grand building – in keeping with the early-twentieth-century wish to promote Muizenberg as a fashionable seaside resort. Complete with clock tower, ticket office, waiting rooms and a tea room, it was opened by the Minister of Railways.

On the same side as the station, No. 153 was the former **post office ㉓** and sorting office, constructed in 1934. The ceramic-tile murals depict ships and were designed and made by the Isa Cameron Ceramic Studio in 1934.

Back on the mountain side is a park where there are two old cannons, reminders of the Battle of Muizenberg that took place here in 1795. Turn left up Camp Street, so named because of the British convalescent camp that operated here between 1900 and 1902 during the Anglo-Boer War.

The **synagogue ㉔**, on the right, was built in 1924 and at one time had a congregation of over 500 families, as well as a surge of summer visitors.

A little further up the street is a path to the **kramat ㉕** of Sayed Abdul Aziz. It is thought he was captured in the Dutch East Indies and brought to the Cape as a slave. From here, return to Main Road, cross over and go down York Road. It is hard to visualise, but 50 years ago this was the main shopping area of the suburb. The railway crossing was open to vehicular traffic and there was a Central News Agency, Cuthberts Shoe Store, Truworths, a dry-cleaner, a pharmacy and a butcher. The shopfronts on one side are original.

Use the pedestrian crossing; on the left is the Kent Stores Building, dating from 1916. Across the road are the colourful bathing huts at Surfers' Corner and the starting point of the walk.

Former whalers' cottages

DISTANCE
± 2 km

TERRAIN
Flat

EFFORT
Easy

USEFUL
INFORMATION
Muizenberg Tourism
021 787 9140

REFRESHMENTS
Coffee shops and cafés along
the route

Muizenberg Village

This walk meanders through the mainly residential area and recalls the past of a neighbourhood that was once home to a bustling Jewish community. Here, in Muizenberg's heyday, there used to be many Jewish-owned hotels and boarding houses that flourished during the summer season.

There are surfboards aplenty at the popular Surfers' Corner, which is also the starting point of this walk.

GILLIAN BLACK

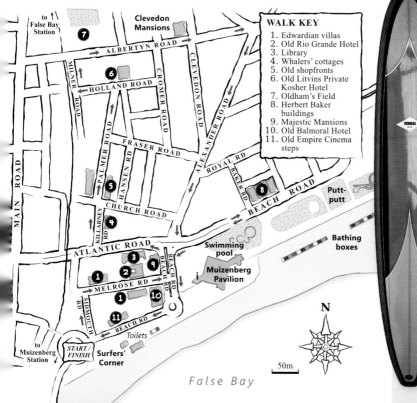

WALK KEY
1. Edwardian villas
2. Old Rio Grande Hotel
3. Library
4. Whalers' cottages
5. Old shopfronts
6. Old Litvins Private Kosher Hotel
7. Oldham's Field
8. Herbert Baker buildings
9. Majestic Mansions
10. Old Balmoral Hotel
11. Old Empire Cinema steps

False Bay

THE WALK

Start at the traffic circle opposite Surfers' Corner at Muizenberg Beach. Cross to the shops and you will see a lane leading to Melrose Road, where there are two groups of double-storey **Edwardian villas ❶**. The former **Rio Grande Hotel ❷** has been converted and now houses an academic institute. During the 1950s, it is claimed Muizenberg had 11 licensed hotels and 10 or more residential hotels or boarding houses.

At the end of Melrose Road, turn left into Beach Road and left again into Atlantic Road. The **library ❸**, on the left, was originally built to house the fire station and electricity department. The Cape Town City Council's crest, which also includes Jan van Riebeeck's coat of arms, appears on the gables of the building. Cross the road and turn right into Killarney Road. The two prefabricated buildings on the right, colourfully restored, were imported from Scandinavia in 1898 as **cottages for whalers ❹** working on the coast beyond Zandvlei.

Take a left and then right turn into Palmer Road. With its colonnades and interesting **old shopfronts ❺**, this section of the street used to be a busy retail area. In the 1950s there was Dankers Clothing Store, a kosher butcher, a dairy, a gents' hairdresser, a shoe repairer, a café and a fruit trader, among others. The rest of the street is residential. Turn left into Holland Road; the Hamburg Bed and Breakfast used to be **Litvins Private Kosher Hotel ❻**, established around 1930. Turn right into Milner Road by the railway. In Albertyn Road, part of a larger field still exists. This area, now known as **Oldham's Field ❼** (named after a local dairy farmer and chemist), was used as the landing site for the first airmail delivery performed in South Africa. On 27 December 1911, a Bleriot monoplane flew from Kenilworth to Oldham's Field in seven and a half minutes carrying a cargo of postcards. A return flight was made to Kenilworth with another bag of mail.

Continue down Albertyn Road and take note of the art deco apartment block before turning right into Clevedon Road. Go along Alexander Road to Beach Road, where there are four **Herbert Baker buildings ❽** facing the sea. The buildings now house the St Leger Retirement Home and the Lindbergh Arts Foundation. Return along Beach Road and turn left. You will see **Majestic Mansions ❾**, which has some art deco details.

The Cape Town City Council crest appears at the entrance to Muizenberg Library.

As you go towards the beach front, the next building you will pass is a local landmark. The former **Balmoral Hotel** ❿ was built in 1932, designed by J. Lonstein in the art deco style. The hotel became a major part of the town's social life; it has been converted into apartments.

Muizenberg's tourism popularity peaked in the two decades after World War II. The second pavilion, built in 1929 to an art deco design by W.H. Grant, was a great attraction. It had a large hall for dancing and entertainment, and a popular tea room drew huge crowds in summer. Every year a special train ran from Johannesburg in December, which shunted at Salt River and went directly to Muizenberg, packed with holidaymakers and their luggage.

By the end of the 1960s, Muizenberg's popularity as a holiday destination was on the wane. A number of factors contributed to this, including competition from Durban for tourists, the closing down of a number of hotels because of hotel grading requirements, the demolition of the pavilion in 1965 for safety reasons and the development of air transport, which made overseas destinations more accessible.

On the way back to the starting point along Beach Road, there is a token attempt to remember the old Empire Cinema in a new development, including a false facade bearing the cinema's name. The **steps** ⓫ at the entrance seem to be from the original building. This concludes a somewhat nostalgic walk.

Houses designed by Sir Herbert Baker along Beach Road in Muizenberg

DISTANCE
3,5 km

TERRAIN
Flat; slope up to
St John's Church

EFFORT
Moderate

**USEFUL
INFORMATION**
Church of St John
the Evangelist
021 761 9020

Wynberg Dutch
Reformed Church
open 8 a.m. to 3 p.m.
021 797 8340

Maynardville Open-
Air Theatre
summer season only
www.artscape.co.za

REFRESHMENTS
■ Café Verdi, Wolfe Street
■ Have a picnic in Wynberg
Park or Maynardville Park

An old telephone
booth still stands
in Wolfe Street.

Little Chelsea

Wynberg

Jan van Riebeeck planted the Cape's first vineyard on the farm De Oude Wijnbergh (The Old Wine Mountain) in the seventeenth century. Today this suburb consists of a number of diverse areas, which are covered by this walk. The charm of the Little Chelsea neighbourhood contrasts with the area bordered by the busy Main Road. A proposed bypass scheme in the 1970s resulted in a swathe of property being acquired by the council, some of which has not been developed to this day.

THE WALK

Begin in the parking area opposite Wynberg Library. The **Methodist Church ❶** in Church Street bears the date 1851. Next to it, the stone cottage is a reminder of what the street would have looked like then. Between the church and the cottage is the grand entrance gate to the Dutch Reformed cemetery. The Masonic **Odd Fellows Hall ❷** at No. 66 opened in 1882 and is the home of the Loyal Victoria Lodge. On the opposite corner, at No. 25, is the old Capital Cinema from 1940, now converted into shops and offices.

Walk along Brodie Road. The open space on the left is the Muslim cemetery. Turn right into Riverstone Road; on the right, on the corner with Main Road is **La Plaisance ❸**, a thatched cottage dating from the 1830s. Turn right into Main Road. Central House on the corner of Main Road and Church Street has an ornate roof profile. Turn left into Lower Maynard Road, and on the left is an art deco building. When it was built, it served as the Electricity Department's showroom and showcased the 'new' electric stoves and

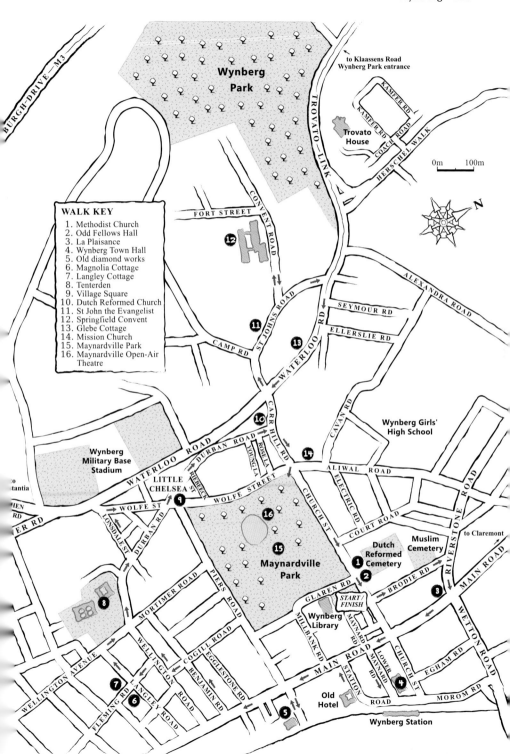

WALK KEY
1. Methodist Church
2. Odd Fellows Hall
3. La Plaisance
4. Wynberg Town Hall
5. Old diamond works
6. Magnolia Cottage
7. Langley Cottage
8. Tenterden
9. Village Square
10. Dutch Reformed Church
11. St John the Evangelist
12. Springfield Convent
13. Glebe Cottage
14. Mission Church
15. Maynardville Park
16. Maynardville Open-Air Theatre

other appliances. This was when households were switching from piped gas and coal stoves to electricity. In the early 1930s, the City Council initiated a 'cook by wire' campaign and introduced a hire-purchase scheme to sell electrical goods.

Wynberg Town Hall ❹, on the next corner, was designed by competition winner W. Black in 1899. It has a flamboyant design, but the encroachment of the surrounding buildings and the taxi rank at the station detract from its style. Walk south and turn into Station Road. Here the former Royal Hotel has a market in the galleried courtyard.

Return to Main Road and turn left. Fifty years ago, Wynberg had at least two department stores here, McDonalds and Duncan & Taylor. On the south corner, opposite Standard Bank, was Rifkin & Miller, a general dealer that advertised that it stocked everything from a needle to an anchor. The shops have changed but the colonnades remain. Turn left at Piers Road; the building at No. 1 used to be a **gemstone- and diamond-cutting works** ❺. The building dates from 1929; on the facade in relief is a cluster of leaves – there used to be a stag's head with antlers, which has been replaced with what looks like a bird's head.

Back on Main Road, at No. 219, on the corner on the south side, is one of city's original milestones marking eight miles from the Old Town House in the city centre (see page 28). Across the road on the left are the tall sides of a warehouse building. This used to be the Gaiety Cinema, which closed down when the Group Areas Act forced a lot of the residents to move. Turn right into Benjamin Road, where most of the cottages have been restored.

Turn left into Coghill Road, right into Wellington Road and then left into Fleming Road. On opposite corners of Langley Road are two interesting thatched cottages. **Magnolia Cottage** ❻, at No. 15, is a rectangular building with a hipped roof. **Langley Cottage** ❼, at No. 17, is smaller and narrower, and dates from around 1825, with some later additions. Continue up Langley Road into Wellington Avenue and turn right. On the left, **Tenterden** ❽ stands in large grounds.

Wynberg Town Hall (top) with lion detail (above) supporting the balcony

The current house has been remodelled a couple of times but dates from circa 1870. It has belonged to the Provincial Government since 1939 and is used as a children's home. Note the single gate pillar on the pavement, which suggests a grander entrance in the past.

Go up Durban Road and turn left into Lonsdale Street, where there are a number of attractive cottages. On the corner is a historical landmark. The double-storey building from 1896 has some great Victorian features, including the fish-scale roof turret, plaster mouldings and stepped end gables; the gryphons adjoining the turret add a grand touch. This was the village bakery, owned at one stage by Attwells Baking Company.

Turn right into Wolfe Street, where there are a couple of old cottages. Nos 7 and 9 form a double-storey business block, dated 1898, that used to be Shaw & Allan's Hardware Store. There is an old telephone booth and an old postbox on Wolfe Street. On the corner of Wolfe Street and Durban Road is the **Village Square** ❾. This area, known as Little Chelsea, is the centre of Wynberg Village. The village developed around the British military camp that formed there. The wagon route to the British naval base at Simon's Town came along Wolfe Street via Aliwal Road. By the early 1820s, a number of cottages had been built, used by army officers and their families. By 1850 there was a thriving community here, with shops, a magistrate and a Dutch and an English church. By the end of the nineteenth century, the centre had shifted to Main Road and the nearby railway line. The village was protected from encroachments by the barrier created by the large private estate of Maynardville. The Wynberg Village Society, which has been in existence for the last 40 years, succeeded in its quest to have the neighbourhood declared an urban conservation area.

The route continues along Durban Road. A number of side streets beckon to be explored. There is a host of cottages along Durban Road,

Ornate turret in Lonsdale Road (above); British-style post box in Wolfe Street (below)

The imposing Wynberg Dutch Reformed Church

many with interesting names. The double-storey building on the corner of Riebeeck Street (Nos 35–43) once housed the municipal offices before the town hall was built. It has also been used as a grocery store and a lodging house. On the opposite corner and fronting onto Waterloo Road is the old Prince Alfred Arms, now a medical practice. It was here that Prince Alfred stopped for refreshment on his journey from Simon's Town to Cape Town to officiate at the ceremony to commence the building of the breakwater and the Alfred Basin (see page 66)

At the end of the road is the **Dutch Reformed Church ⑩**. The original church was built in 1831; it underwent major renovations in 1897/8. The clock is German and dated 1882.

From here there is a choice of two routes: either continue up the hill to St John's Church and Springfield Convent, or go down Church Street to the starting point after visiting Maynardville Park.

Go up Carr Hill Road, cross Waterloo Road and continue into St John's Terrace. The Anglican church of **St John the Evangelist ⑪** is an impressive stone-built example of the Cape Victorian neo-Gothic style. The interior shows its connection to the Wynberg military base during the British colonial era in the Cape. Further on is the **Springfield Convent of the Holy Rosary ⑫**, an independent Catholic girls' school. The hub of the institution is Springfield House, the original convent building, which had a second storey added in 1871. The name comes from the Krakeelwater spring, which runs through the property. The stone-built St Anne's pre-primary school was added in 1895.

Turn right onto Waterloo Road. **Glebe Cottage ⑬**, about 150 metres along on the right, is a lovely thatched Cape long house. Built around 1800, it has had many uses: officers' mess, hospital, storeroom, post office, Anglican chapel and church school. In 1841 there was a classroom on these premises – the origin of Wynberg Boys' School. It is now privately owned. Across the road there is an old aloe tree on the remaining section of Waterloo Green.

Go down Carr Hill Road to its intersection with Aliwal Road. On the left in Aliwal is **Mission Church** ⑭, built in 1881 after the Wynberg Dutch Reformed Church divided its congregation along racial lines. Various additions, including the bell tower, were made over the years.

At the corner of Church and Wolfe streets is the entrance to **Maynardville Park** ⑮. The Maynard family came to the Cape with the British settlers in 1820. A son, James, and his sister were among the early residents of Wynberg Village. James was a successful businessman, shareholder of the Wynberg Railway and member of the Cape Legislative Assembly. He acquired a large portion of land and named the property Maynardville. He died in 1874, and his nephew, William Maynard Farmer, inherited the property. William was married to the daughter of Major Wolfe, the magistrate of Wynberg (after whom Wolfe Street is named). He was very successful in the early days of the diamond industry and it was at this time that the glories of the Maynardville estate were added. The house was extended to form a large double-storey homestead. William Maynard brought a gardener, Robert Bain, from England who had trained at Kew Gardens. The sunken garden, archery lawn, and extensive beds of hydrangeas and oleanders stem from this time. The Krakeelwater stream forms a large pond, which is a feature of the park. Cape Town's high society, including bishops, generals, admirals and gentry, swept up the driveway in their carriages, past the gates made from Napoleon's tomb in St Helena (which have since been returned to the island) to attend parties here. When the last relative died in 1949, the property was offered to Cape Town City Council, which purchased it for use as a public park. The house was demolished but the layout of the gardens and many trees remain.

The **Maynardville Open-Air Theatre** ⑯ is known for its annual staging of Shakespeare plays. Actresses René Ahrenson and Cecelia Sonnenberg started the tradition in 1955. There is a statue of Shakespeare in the theatre grounds.

From here continue along Church Street to the parking area.

WYNBERG PARK

Created in the 1890s as part of the International Park Building Movement, the initiative of local resident William Horne and Wynberg councillor William Morom, it was originally called King Edward Park. Designed with formal flower beds, the park used to have a bandstand and a tea room. The Krakeelwater stream rises here.

The rolling lawns and long-established trees provide an attractive setting. The park has a children's play area, a duck pond and braai (barbeque) facilities. A group of trees was planted by the Guild of Loyal Women in 1902, and 90 years later the Victoria League planted another group. The fountain near the top of Waterloo Road recalls the Coronation of King Edward VII and Queen Alexandra on 9 August 1902.

Directions: Access is now only possible by road. From Waterloo Road/Trovato Link, turn into Klaassens Road and then into 58th Avenue, which leads to the park.

DISTANCE
2 km

TERRAIN
Flat

EFFORT
Easy

USEFUL INFORMATION

Arderne Gardens
open daily 8 a.m. to 5 p.m.

Cavendish Square Shopping Centre
for paid parking, toilets and refreshments
www.cavendish.co.za

Grove Primary School
for a close-up view of the Herschel Obelisk – school terms only
021 674 2077

Montebello Design Centre
021 685 6445
www.montebello@telkomsa.net

Vineyard Hotel
021 657 4500
www.vineyard.co.za

REFRESHMENTS

- Cavendish Square Shopping Centre (restaurants and cafés)
- The Gardener's Cottage Restaurant at Montebello: 021 689 3158
- Two restaurants at the Vineyard Hotel & Spa; the Splash Café is open in summer only

Vineyard Hotel

Claremont

When you walk around the southern suburb of Claremont today, it is hard to imagine that 150 years or so ago the area consisted of large country estates on either side of Main Road. This walk visits some of the buildings of that period. The arrival of the railway station in 1864, the first intermediate stop between Salt River and Wynberg, helped develop the commercial shopping area that exists today.

The name of the suburb comes from Claremont House, the home of Sir John Molteno, who was appointed as the first prime minister of the Cape Colony in 1872.

THE WALK

Start from Cavendish Square Shopping Centre, which provides parking, refreshments and toilets.

Exit onto Cavendish Street on the mountain side. Cross the road, turn left, and after a few metres turn up Obelisk Way and turn right into Ingle Road – a narrow street of small cottages. A number of residents were forced to move from this area under the Group Areas Act. At the end of the street, on the corner of Vineyard and Quiet streets, is **Old Thatch Cottage ❶**, dating from 1860 and still in good condition.

Return along Quiet Street to Bishoplea Road and walk towards the mountain to the corner of Feldhausen Avenue. The **tombs ❷** of Baroness Frierke von Buschenröder (died 1831) and her daughter (died 1827), who was married to J.B.C. Knobel, the surveyor general, are visible through the fence. The Feldhausen estate was large and covered the area where Grove Primary School is today, and extended as far as Herschel Girls' School.

Continue up and around the school into Morris Road and then turn left into Grove Avenue. If you look through the gates of the school you will see the **Herschel Obelisk** ❸. Sir John Herschel, the son of Sir William – both astronomers – came to the Cape in 1834 to observe the southern skies. He brought with him a six-metre reflecting telescope. He bought Feldhausen in 1835. He allowed the original owners to stay on part of the estate and in gratitude they named that portion 'Herschel'. He drew sketches of the Cape and recorded varieties of local wild flowers. He also played an active part in the Cape education system. Herschel returned to England in 1838. The obelisk, which was imported from England, was erected in 1841.

VINEYARD HOTEL

This is where Andrew and Lady Anne Barnard had their country residence in 1800. Lady Anne Barnard describes the area in her diary as 'surrounded by the largest field of vines in Africa' (it was 10 acres). The Georgian two-storey, five-bay section (circa 1850) is on the site of the original building and has a fountain rescued from Westerford, an old house that was demolished. The old part of the hotel retains its mid-nineteenth-century feel. The Lady Anne Gallery has a pictorial display of the time she spent at the Cape. The gardens are beautifully maintained and well worth the visit.

Directions: Driving from the Cavendish Square parking area, take the Vineyard Road exit. From Vineyard Road turn right into Cavendish Street. Cross Protea Road into Kildare Road. Turn left into Colinton Road, and the hotel is on the right.

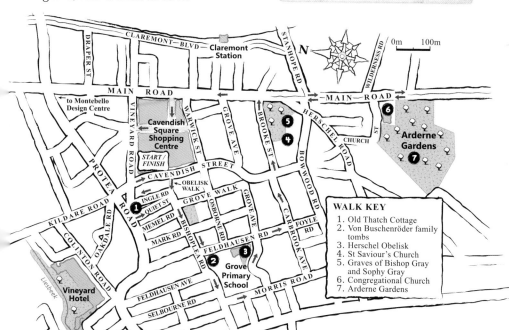

WALK KEY
1. Old Thatch Cottage
2. Von Buschenröder family tombs
3. Herschel Obelisk
4. St Saviour's Church
5. Graves of Bishop Gray and Sophy Gray
6. Congregational Church
7. Arderne Gardens

Continue to Foyle Road, turn right and then left into Carbrook Avenue, and then into Brooke Street. The foundation stone of **St Saviour's Church ❹**, on the right-hand side, was laid in 1850. The first service was held on Easter Sunday, 27 March 1853. The church was designed by Bishop Gray's wife, Sophy. She visited the building site daily from their home in Bishopscourt. The impressive bell tower with its three bells is the work of English architect W. Butterfield, and was completed in 1880. Sir Herbert Baker made further additions in 1903 and used imported Bath stone. The **graves ❺** of the bishop and his wife, as well as a memorial with a map of the Gray churches, are in the graveyard, close to the church on the Main Road side. The Bishop and his wife designed more than 40 churches and chapels in South Africa. They travelled extensively to develop congregations around the Cape.

Turn right into Main Road, and the next church is the lovely thatched **Congregational Church ❻**, built on land given by the Arderne family, who owned what are now the Arderne Gardens. The cornerstone is dated 1840 but most of the present-day church was built in 1892.

This pretty thatched Congregational Church is situated on Main Road

MONTEBELLO DESIGN CENTRE

One of the large estates in the area was Montebello, on Newlands Avenue. When the grounds and house were sold in the 1950s for the development of SACS school, the old stables in a corner of the grounds were retained. The main house, with its ballroom, is now used as a school boarding house.

Cecil Michaelis, son of Sir Max Michaelis, arranged for the stable section to be used as a design centre. This houses a large variety of art and craft studios and workshops. The old stable buildings have an attractive design, complete with clock, and there are several original features and fixtures.

In the conservatory, attached to the nursery, is a bust of Cecil Michaelis. His father donated his collection of paintings, which can be seen in the Old Town House, Greenmarket Square (see page 28).

Before leaving, have a look at the gates with the name Montebello, custom-made by Coalbrookdale Foundry in England.

Directions: From Main Road, Claremont, continue towards Cape Town. At Dean Street, turn towards the mountain and at the Newlands Avenue intersection turn left; Montebello is on the left.

Bust of Cecil Michaelis

Next door to the church are the public **Arderne Gardens ❼**. Known originally as the Hill, the land was bought in 1845 by Ralph Henry Arderne, a collector of rare plants who was in correspondence with the curator of Kew Gardens in London. Arderne developed a private botanic garden on the property. His son, Henry Mathew, shared his father's interest in the garden. It is said he often asked ship captains travelling to foreign parts to bring him seeds and plants. The City Council purchased the land in 1927 and opened it to the public. The gardens contain an interesting collection of trees and an attractive shrubbery. A Friends of the Arderne Gardens group was formed in 2004; it organises volunteers to work in and guide people around the gardens and maintains an information board in the garden. From here, retrace your route back to Cavendish Square.

The Arderne Gardens stock an interesting collection of trees.

Liesbeek River

This stained-glass window graces the Rondebosch Library.

Liesbeek River Trail

This is one of Cape Town's best-kept secrets. The route follows the river along its shady banks before returning along Main Road. The Liesbeek River has its source above Kirstenbosch National Botanical Garden and runs for 13 kilometres to the sea, near Salt River. It is crossed by 35 bridges. The river formed a natural boundary of the early settlement and was originally known as the Fresh River, and then the Amstel (after the river in Amsterdam). In 1657 Van Riebeeck named it the Liesbeeq (in early Dutch, *lies* is reeds and *beeq* a stream).

This walk is ideal in summer, as it is cool and sheltered.

THE WALK

Start at the old **Rondebosch Town Hall** ❶ in Belmont Road, built in 1900 for the Rondebosch Municipality before it was incorporated into Cape Town in 1913. This building, designed by G.M. Alexander, has a stained-glass window depicting the crest of the Rondebosch Municipality. It is now a library.

Go up Belmont Road towards the mountain. On the left-hand side of the road bridge is the start of the Liesbeek River Trail. Old stonework can be seen underneath the bridge. Follow the canalised river as far as Rouwkoop Road; **St Michael's Catholic Church** ❷ is on the left-hand side. This began as a mission church in 1853. The first building was damaged by the Liesbeek flooding, which meant the church had to be rebuilt further away from the riverbank. The area was called

Groeneveld (Green Fields) and some of the 11 free burghers (see page 6) were granted farms here in 1657. 'Rouwkoop' means the money paid to release a party from a contract, in other words forfeit money. The free burghers had a contract with the VOC to farm and provide produce at a fixed price.

The trail continues across the road to the little bridge with rails. Make a detour here: turn right and a few metres along there is an opening in the wall that runs into the cul-de-sac Bank Road. On the left is the **Albion Spring** ❸ pump house. Continue a few more metres and look back at the Schweppes emblem on the wall. In 1888 the Dix brothers established the Excelsior Ice and Mineral Water Factory using water from the spring. This became the factory of Schweppes

The Schweppes emblem is on the wall of the Albion Spring pump house.

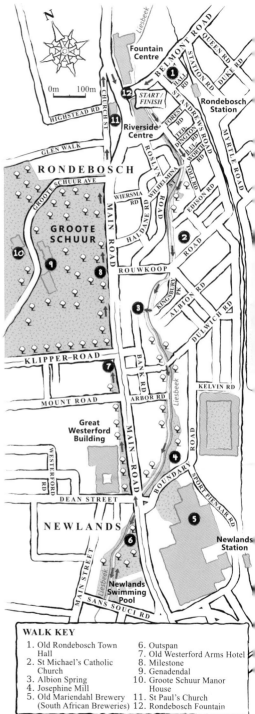

WALK KEY

1. Old Rondebosch Town Hall
2. St Michael's Catholic Church
3. Albion Spring
4. Josephine Mill
5. Old Mariendahl Brewery (South African Breweries)
6. Outspan
7. Old Westerford Arms Hotel
8. Milestone
9. Genadendal
10. Groote Schuur Manor House
11. St Paul's Church
12. Rondebosch Fountain

Josephine Mill, built in 1840, was restored to full working order in 1988.

Mineral Waters until it was demolished in the 1970s. There is a terrace of double-storey Georgian buildings, now used as offices. In the corner, next to the passage entrance, is the two-storey Albion Lodge, previously the water manager's house, now in use as an Abbeyfield home for the aged. Return to the walkway.

The **Josephine Mill** ❹ was built in 1840 by Jacob Letterstedt, a Swede, and named after the crown princess of Sweden. It was restored by the Cape Town Historical Society in 1988. The large water wheel can be glimpsed through the trees. The trail goes under Westerford Bridge.

Cross Dean Street and a short walk along Main Road will bring you to the next section of the walk. Opposite and across Main Road is South African Breweries, where several famous beer brands are made. The old **Mariendahl Brewery** ❺ on the same site dates from 1859. Now part of South African Breweries, it is open for tours and has a heritage museum. Tours have to be booked in advance.

Proceed along the trail. The parking area on the left was originally an **outspan** ❻ where ox wagons and horse-drawn vehicles could rest on their journey from Cape Town to Simon's Town. The riverbanks here are steep and natural. The path terminates at Sans Souci Road. Retrace your steps to Main Road and walk along the shaded left-hand side towards Rondebosch. On the left is the Westerford Office Park, built originally for an insurance company. Opposite is the Cape Peninsula Old Aged Society's head office – on the facade is the emblem of the Masonic Hall.

The large two-storey building on the corner of Klipper Road, at No. 230, used to be the site of the **Westerford Arms Hotel** ❼. The hotel was built circa 1885, and became one of the many hotels and off-sales units of the old Ohlsson's Brewery, the predecessor of South African Breweries.

Along Main Road, opposite Rouwkoop Road, is an original **milestone** ❽ from around 1830. The Roman numeral 'V' is carved on the Robben Island slate stone, denoting a distance of five miles from the Old Town House on Greenmarket Square.

Behind high security fences is **Genadendal** ❾ (formerly Westbrooke), a house used by presidents of the republic. The house dates from 1832, though it has been extensively altered a number of times.

The **Groote Schuur Manor House** ❿ used to be the prime minister's dwelling. The house and estate were given to the government by Cecil John Rhodes, who employed Sir Herbert Baker to remodel the house. This was the architect's first major project in South Africa. It was rebuilt after a fire in 1896. The church on the hill, **St Paul's Anglican Church** ⓫, was designed by Charles Michell, the surveyor general, and built from 1832 to 1834. Michell also designed Sir Lowry's Pass over the Hottentots Holland Mountains and Michell's Pass at Ceres.

Cross Main Road at St Paul's Church and have a look at the **Rondebosch Fountain** ⓬ on the corner of Main and Belmont roads. It was made in Glasgow by Walter Macfarlane & Co., and is a typical example of Victorian ironmongery. It was given to the citizens of Rondebosch by George Moodie, who owned Westbrooke at the time. The legs are in the form of a horse's hooves and support the trough from which horses could slake their thirst. The arms held cups for people to drink from and at the base, now missing, were bowls for dogs. The light on top, with its fish-scale pattern, was powered by electricity from the generator at Westbrooke, making it, arguably, the first electric street light in Cape Town.

Made in Glasgow – the Rondebosch Fountain is a typical example of Victorian ironmongery.

This concludes the walk. However, the path continues on the station side of the river to Rosebank. This is not recommended, though, as it is isolated, flat and uninteresting. See also the Liesbeek River Walk (page 134) for a different exploration around the Liesbeek River.

DISTANCE
3 km

TERRAIN
Flat; incline
over railway
bridge; steps at
the Rosebank
and Observatory
stations

EFFORT
Easy

**USEFUL
INFORMATION**
**Heart of Cape Town
Museum**
admission charge;
tours 7 days a week:
9am, 11am, 1pm & 3pm
021 404 1967
www.heartofcapetown.co.za

**South African
Astronomical
Observatory**
open on certain
Saturday nights
021 447 0025
www.saao.ac.za

REFRESHMENTS
Several cafés and bars on
Lower Main Road, Observatory

Valkenberg Manor House, Observatory

Liesbeek River Walk

This walk follows the Liesbeek River between Rosebank and Observatory stations, and you can reach the start by means of the Metro Rail southern-suburbs train service. The route is exposed to the elements so use protection against the wind and sun. It is also isolated in parts so it is recommended that companions be sought for this stroll.

THE WALK

Start at **Rosebank Station** ❶ on the side away from the mountain. Walk along Lower Nursery Road towards Cape Town and turn right into Alma Road, which leads to Liesbeek Parkway. Cross over and on the left the path follows the river, which is canalised at this part.

With the heavy traffic on this dual carriageway, it is hard to imagine that 350 years ago this was the farmland of the free burghers (see page 61). Here they grew wheat and vegetables, and raised poultry and animals to provide the VOC ships with fresh produce. It was a hard life, as they had to cope with wild animals, such as lion, leopard and hyena, which attacked their livestock. Furthermore, the Khoikhoi were unhappy with having their land taken from them and raided the

Bird life thrives along the Liesbeek River.

settlers' land. There were two farms here in the late 1770s: Rijgersdal spanned both sides of the river, and Vredenburg went as far as Klipfontein Road. The farmhouse, much altered, is still there but cannot be seen from the river it used to face. The path crosses Klipfontein Road, and on the right are the playing fields of St George's Grammar School. This was part of Bloemendal Farm. An old thatched house dating from the early 1800s is still on the school grounds.

Sometimes people fish where the river opens up here. Once under the Settlers Way Bridge, you will get a glimpse of Coornhoop (Hope of Corn) on the left. Only the pigeon loft and the restored barns remain. Historically, this was one of the main wheat-growing areas. Van Riebeeck built a small fort here, to protect the early farmers, and a barn.

Along the river, the free burghers were allowed to fish. In his diary of 1660, Van Riebeeck records that one of them caught an eel 'twice as thick as a man's arm, fleshy and tasty'.

And it was along here that a VOC patrolman had to be rescued from a tree that he had climbed to avoid the attentions of a lion splashing in the shallows of the river.

This is one of the most attractive sections of the river, and the walking path, newly developed by the City of Cape Town, comes close to the river in places. On the mountain side are some hockey fields and Hartleyvale Stadium, which was home to the Cape Town City soccer team in the 1960s and 1970s.

WALK KEY

1. Rosebank Station
2. South African Astronomical Observatory
3. World War I memorial
4. Heart of Cape Town Museum
5. Observatory Station

The Observatory war memorial

Visible on the right-hand side, just past the junction of Station Road and Liesbeek Parkway, Observatory, is the **South African Astronomical Observatory ②**, which can be accessed from Observatory Road. In 1820 the British Admiralty in London decided to establish an astronomical observatory in the southern hemisphere. The site between the Liesbeek and Black rivers has a slight incline. The first buildings were built in 1825/6. The site was part of the then Valkenberg Farm, which was one of the largest along the river.

Walk up Station Road towards the mountain. Over the railway bridge on the right-hand side is a new square where a **World War I memorial ③** has been re-erected from its previous site on Hospital Bend. The inscription on the base reads: 'Build well on the foundations laid by their great sacrifice.' Plaques list the names of the residents of the suburb killed in the war. Originally known as Observatory Road, this area developed into a dense residential area once the railway was opened. Today, Observatory is a busy suburb with a bohemian character and has a strong connection with the university and Groote Schuur Hospital.

HEART OF CAPE TOWN MUSEUM

On 3 December 1967, Professor Christiaan Barnard performed the world's first successful heart transplant at Cape Town's Groote Schuur Hospital. The operation was considered a medical milestone and, as a result, the hospital received international recognition. The **Heart of Cape Town Museum ④**, which recalls this event, offers tours of the theatre and wards where the transplant took place.

Groote Schuur Hospital was completed in 1936. It was not designed by Sir Herbert Baker, as is generally believed, but by J.S. Clelland, who was secretary of the Public Works Department. He commissioned a number of artists and craftsmen to contribute to the embellishment of the new building. Born in Woodstock, sculptor Ernest Quilter created a number of works depicting Greek mythological characters on the facade. The bas-relief elements for the side pediments were created by Ethelwynne Quail of Cape Town. The intricately carved doors and fanlights are the work of Vladimir Meyerowitz, who taught sculpting and wood carving at the UCT School of Fine Arts. (He and his students also carved the entrance doors of the Iziko South African National Gallery in the Company's Garden.) In the front garden are two stone benches with lion masques designed by Ivan Mitford-Barberton. The new maternity block, built in the 1960s, has mouldings of storks, a symbol of childbirth.

Directions: The old Groote Schuur Building can be reached by going up Station Road from **Observatory Station ⑤** and continuing up Groote Schuur Drive.

Rhodes Recreation Ground

Mowbray

Mowbray was the name given to this southern suburb in 1850, when a group of residents petitioned the Cape governor to change the name from Drie Koppen (see page 138). Mowbray Hall was a large house built in 1828 on the main road, named after Melton Mowbray in England.

As well as the old Mostert's Mill, this suburb has a charming collection of free-standing Victorian houses. Today Mowbray has a large student population.

(see page 138)

DISTANCE
2,5 km

TERRAIN
Steep slope to
Mostert's Mill

EFFORT
Moderate

USEFUL INFORMATION
Irma Stern Museum
021 685 5686
www.irmastern.co.za

Mostert's Mill
open certain Saturdays
088 129 7168

Shoprite Mowbray on Main
Road has parking

REFRESHMENTS
Cafés on Main Road

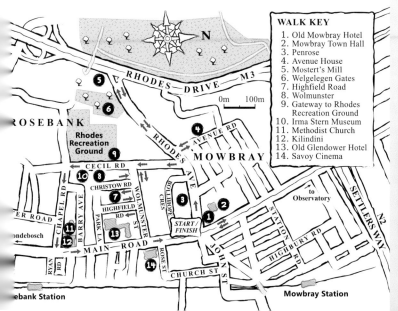

WALK KEY
1. Old Mowbray Hotel
2. Mowbray Town Hall
3. Penrose
4. Avenue House
5. Mostert's Mill
6. Welgelegen Gates
7. Highfield Road
8. Wolmunster
9. Gateway to Rhodes Recreation Ground
10. Irma Stern Museum
11. Methodist Church
12. Kilindini
13. Old Glendower Hotel
14. Savoy Cinema

Mostert's Mill was built in 1796 and first restored in 1935 and again in 1995.

GILLIAN BLACK

THE WALK

Start on the busy corner of Main Road and Rhodes Avenue. The building on the corner of Rhodes Avenue was known as the **Mowbray Hotel ❶**, and was formerly one of the old Ohlsson's Brewery hotels. Much altered over time, the structure dates from 1870. It is now used by the University of Cape Town.

This corner hosted its first tavern in 1697, and in 1724 it was given the name Drie Koppen (Three Heads) as a result of a murder committed here by three slaves. They were beheaded for their crime, and their heads placed on stakes as a deterrent to passers-by. After that, the area became known as Drie Koppen. However, during the British occupation this was incorrectly translated as Three Cups. After a petition by residents, the name was changed to Mowbray.

Diagonally opposite is a double-storey building with attics dating from 1903. For many years this was the depot of a dry-cleaning firm. Across the road is the Schachs Building and a group

The Mowbray Town Hall was built in 1900.

of commercial buildings circa 1900. The Schach family used to own the Mowbray bottle store. As the residential neighbourhood of Pinelands developed in the 1950s, and was lacking in shops, Mowbray businesses flourished – butchers, fisheries and the bottle store supplied Pinelanders with their provisions.

Just beyond the old Mowbray Hotel on Main Road is **Mowbray Town Hall ❷**. Designed by architects Tully & Waters, it was built in 1900 and has a domed belfry. Mowbray was a separate municipality from 1890 until approximately 1910, when it was incorporated into Cape Town. Note the crest, which includes three heads and three cups! Welgelegen was the name of a farm that used to be in this area.

Now head back to Rhodes Avenue. On the left as you head

up towards the mountain, at No. 9 is **Penrose ❸**, a well-restored double-storey Victorian house, circa 1902, with cast-iron veranda supports and an attractive balcony.

Further on the right is Avenue Road, with **Avenue House ❹** (circa 1895), formerly the Chinese School and now restored by UCT, as is Cadboll, next door.

Return to Rhodes Avenue and go up the hill to **Mostert's Mill ❺**. Welgelegen belonged to Dirk van Reenen, whose son-in-law, Wybrand Mostert, built the Mill in 1796. Its thatched cap rotates to face the wind. The round threshing floor is on the left of the property, next to a display of millstones and explanation boards. The miller's house next door is called De Meule (The Mill) and is now a government residence that has been extensively renovated.

One of a number of elegant Victorian houses in Mowbray

The **gates ❻** to the old Welgelegen Farm are on Rhodes Avenue. The farm extended up the slopes of Table Mountain. Most of the upper part of Mowbray is laid out either on the former site of Welgelegen or the adjoining farm, Zorgvliet (where the College of Music is now located). Both farms were bought by Cecil John Rhodes and bequeathed to the nation. The current building, Welgelegen, was designed by Sir Herbert Baker and is part of the university.

As you descend the slope, turn right into Cecil Road (named after Rhodes) and left into Wolmunster Road, which has a couple of Victorian villas, and turn right into **Highfield Road ❼**, which has an interesting selection of free-standing Victorian buildings, the pick of which is No. 6 – a double-storey house, which has unfortunately lost its balcony.

Return and turn left, and then left again into Christow Road. No. 8 is **Wolmunster ❽**, named after the French town on the German border. Built in 1836, this is one of the original estates that stretched between Cecil Road and Main Road. It was built for Attorney General William Porter.

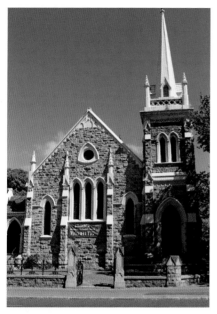

Go up Wolmunster and left into Cecil Road. The ornate **iron gate** ❾, made in London around 1900, is the entrance to the Rhodes Recreation Ground.

No. 17 Cecil Road (the Firs) is now the **Irma Stern Museum** ❿. This house dates from 1842, and the second floor was added by architect John Parker in 1904. Leading South African artist Irma Stern bought the house in 1927. The museum houses many of her works and collections. Around the house you will find personal touches of the artist, such as a painted cupboard or a tile. Her studio is as she left it. Outside, now on the side of the house, is the original front entrance with a carved door Stern brought back from Zanzibar.

Go down Chapel Road and note the original driveway entrance to the Firs. Further down on the left, set back from the road, is the imposing **Methodist Church** ⓫ (1899–1900), designed in the Gothic Revival style by architect H.T. Jones. Hodgson Hall (1845) was the original church. Shaw Hall was built as a school. The double-storey Deanery was built as the manse circa 1900. It has an unusual tiled tableau between the windows.

The Rosebank Methodist Church (top), and the the Deanery in the church grounds (above)

On the corner with Main Road is **Kilindini** ⓬, built in 1850. This was a boarding house for many years and is now a UCT hall of residence.

The old **Glendower Hotel** ⓭, in its day a popular suburban hotel, and now also a UCT residence, contains the core of the original Mowbray Hall, whence the suburb gets its name. The covered stoep (veranda), inside fanlight and upstairs windows were part of the hall.

Finally, across Main Road on the corner of Rose Street is the former Savoy Café, which was part of the **Savoy Cinema** ⓮ complex. The building has been altered considerably. The Savoy was designed by W.H. Grant in 1937 for African Consolidated Theatres as a suburban cinema. It was a sister cinema to the Scala in Claremont. In its latter days, it became a Cinerama Theatre, but the growing popularity of television led to its closure.

The Mead

DISTANCE
2,5 km

TERRAIN
Steps over
railway bridge

EFFORT
Easy

**USEFUL
INFORMATION**
St Stephen's Church
021 531 3350

REFRESHMENTS
Millstone Farm Stall
and Café
open Tuesday to Sunday
021 447 8226

Pinelands

Pinelands was South Africa's first garden city. Garden cities were first advocated by Sir Ebenezer Howard in England around the beginning of the twentieth century. His concept proposed spacious, carefully laid-out suburbs with sports facilities and amenities, and required architectural control to maintain good standards and safety precautions for traffic.

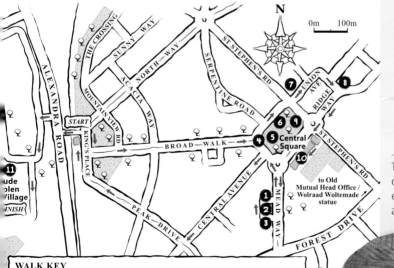

This old millstone can be seen at the eponymous farm stall and café.

WALK KEY

1. The Mead
2. Heritage site plaques
3. Postbox
4. Founding stone
5. Cannon
6. *Southern Floe* commemorative stone
7. St Stephen's Chapel
8. Methodist Chapel
9. Memorial gateway
10. Pinelands Co-operative Society
11. Millstone Farm Stall and Café

Two heritage site plaques (above) and an old postbox (below) can be found on The Mead.

Richard Stuttaford of the well-known South African merchant family started the Garden Cities Trust, a non-profit company, with a personal donation of £10 000 in 1918. Pinelands was the site of the former forestry estate of Uitvlugt donated by the state. The original layout plan for Pinelands was prepared in London in 1919 by architects Thompson, Hennell & James, who were associated with two garden-city schemes in Great Britain.

Although the suburb is only 90 years old, Pinelands has a style and presence of its own. This walk concentrates on what the locals call the 'old part'. The 'new part', further down Forest Drive, was mainly developed after World War II.

THE WALK

Start at Pinelands Station and walk down Broad Walk away from the mountain to Central Square, which is actually a garden. Immediately the spacious layout is noticeable, as are the trees lining the road. On reaching Central Square, turn right and then right again into Mead Way. On the right is **The Mead ❶**; No. 3 was the first house completed in Pinelands, in 1923.

A number of the early houses incorporated thatched roofs in their design. There are two **heritage site plaques ❷** giving details of some of the history of Pinelands. While on The Mead, have a look at the **old postbox ❸** on the grassed area in the middle.

From here, return to Central Square and turn left. Walk towards the Dutch Reformed Church, and on the right there is a **founding stone ❹** laid by General Jan Smuts in May 1923. There used to be a sundial on top but this has disappeared. In the square is an old **cannon ❺** excavated during building work. A **commemorative stone ❻** recalls the crew of HMSAS *Southern Floe*, who were lost on 11 February 1941 off Tobruk, Libya, during a World War II siege.

Where St Stephen's Road connects with Central Square is the St Stephen's Anglican Church. Behind the church is the original thatched **chapel ❼**, built in 1926, when it was opened by the Earl of Athlone, the governor general. It was restored in 1971. At the back of the property is a small garden of remembrance.

The chapel of St Stephen's Anglican Church was built in 1926.

Past the Girl Guides' Hall and behind the municipal offices on Union Avenue is the **Methodist Chapel ❽**, built in 1932. On the next corner of St Stephen's Road is the old police station.

Return to the square; you will see a **memorial gateway ❾** erected in 1960 in memory of the residents who fell in World War II. The supermarket is on the site where the **Pinelands Co-operative Society ❿** started. Return to the station along Central Avenue and take a right turn into Peak Drive. This will give a further opportunity to appreciate the intentions of the original planning scheme.

Cross the railway bridge and turn left and then right into the Oude Molen Eco Village. This rather run-down ex-government institution has been taken over by an enthusiastic group of environmentalists and craft workers. Look out for the **Millstone Farm Stall and Café ⓫**, in the left-hand corner of the village. The Millstone Café is in an old cottage and offers home-made organic food, preserves and delicious breads. There is seating in the rustic garden area around an original millstone and a children's play area. One of the activities here is horse riding. Hopefully, this 'village' will develop when more funding is found.

WOLRAAD WOLTEMADE

The only memorial to the Cape's best-known folk hero is a statue by sculptor Ivan Mitford-Barberton in front of the head office of the Old Mutual in Pinelands. The life story of Wolraad Woltemade is by no means clear. He was a German in the employ of the VOC. It is believed at one time he was keeper of the menagerie at the top of the Government Avenue in Gardens (see page 15). Later he worked as a dairyman on the company's farm near Salt River.

During the early hours of 1 June 1773, strong winds that had been blowing in Table Bay intensified to gale force. *Jonge Thomas*, one of four VOC ships preparing to sail to Holland, went adrift and ran aground at Woodstock Beach. The officials of the company were more interested in saving the valuable cargo than the plight of the shipwrecked sailors. Woltemade was riding past on his horse Vonk (Sparkle) when he heard cries for help. He decided to make his horse swim to the wreck, got two seamen to hold on to the horse's tail and managed to take them ashore. He did this seven times, saving 14 men. Spurred on by the cries of distress, he and his exhausted horse rode into the waves once again. This time, more desperate crew clung to the horse, pulling the brave animal and its rider under and drowning the entire group. In total, 150 drowned; 67 survived the wreck, including the 14 saved by Woltemade. A petition was made to the Dutch authorities about his brave action. The VOC named a ship *Die Held Woltemade* (*The Hero Woltemade*) and granted an annuity to his wife.

Directions: Go down Forest Drive and turn left into Jan Smuts Drive. The statue is at the main entrance to the Old Mutual head office.

Chapman's Peak Drive
SHAEN ADEY/IOA

DRIVES

USEFUL INFORMATION

Boulders Beach
admission charge to penguin colony
021 786 2329
www.tmnp.co.za

Cape of Good Hope Nature Reserve
admission charge at Cape Point
021 780 9010/1
www.capepoint.co.za

Groot Constantia
admission charge to manor house
021 794 5128
www.grootconstantia.co.za

Kirstenbosch National Botanical Garden
admission charge
021 762 0687
www.sanbi.org

Rhodes Memorial
021 689 9151
www.rhodesmemorial.co.za

Table Mountain Cableway
admission charge
021 424 8181
www.tablemountain.net

Table Mountain National Park
admission charge to Silvermine
021 712 7471
www.tmnp.co.za

SHAEN ADEY/IOA

Victoria Drive, Oudekraal

The Grand Drive

A problem with which Capetonians are frequently confronted is what to do with guests who are in Cape Town for just a day or two and want to see everything. Depending on their interests and exactly how long they have, the solution is to take them on the Grand Drive around Cape Town and the Cape Peninsula on the first day and on a visit to Robben Island and the Stellenbosch Winelands on the second.

The drive starts at the Table Mountain Cableway and takes you through Camps Bay and Hout Bay to Noordhoek, via the spectacular Chapman's Peak Drive, and along the coast to Cape Point. The return journey takes you past the penguin colony at Boulders, before continuing through Simon's Town and past the Silvermine section of Table Mountain National Park. From there, the route takes you to Groot Constantia, Kirstenbosch National Botanical Garden and Rhodes Memorial.

Start early on this drive, then you can enjoy breakfast on top of Table Mountain or in Camps Bay. Regular stops are recommended along the route, and perhaps lunch and a tea break. Both Kirstenbosch and the Rhodes Memorial close at sunset. As the day progresses, you can assess your passengers' interests and adjust your plans accordingly.

THE DRIVE

Plan to be on one of the first morning cable cars ❶ going up Table Mountain. Remember, it can be cold on the summit. If the cableway is not operating, drive along Signal Hill Road to the viewing point on **Signal Hill** ❷, overlooking Green Point. On the return journey, make a brief stop at the kramat (burial place) of Sheikh Mohamed Hassen Ghaibie Shah, a learned teacher of Islam. From here, drive down Kloof Road through the Glen and The Roundhouse, and turn left down to Victoria Road and drive along Camps Bay beach front (see page 88).

Along the left-hand side of the drive south to Hout Bay are the mountains known as the Twelve Apostles, thus named by Sir Rufane Donkin, acting governor of the Cape. Shortly after the turn-off to Llandudno, the next road on the left-hand side leads to the Suikerbossie Restaurant. On the bend there is a plaque dedicated to Thomas Bain, 1830–1893, who built Victoria Road, which was his last work. Bain engineered 20 passes and bridges. He was the son of Andrew Bain (who built Bain's Kloof and other passes).

In **Hout Bay** ❸, turn left along Victoria Road to the circle at Imizamo Yethu informal settlement, then turn right along Main Road past Kronendal, Hout Bay's original farm. Built in 1800, the house has preserved its main features through the ages.

The anchors on the Main Road are from the wreck of the SS *Maori*, which sank after hitting rocks at Duikerpoint in 1909.

Towards the end of the road, the Hout Bay Manor Hotel incorporates part of the old Royal Hotel, built in 1871. The Chapman's Peak Hotel is from

DRIVE KEY

1. Table Mountain Cableway
2. Signal Hill
3. Hout Bay
4. Chapman's Peak Drive
5. East Fort
6. Camel Rock
7. Cape of Good Hope Nature Reserve (Cape Point)
8. Boulders (penguin colony)
9. Simon's Town
10. Silvermine
11. Groot Constantia
12. Kirstenbosch National Botanical Garden
13. Rhodes Memorial

0m   5km

REFRESHMENTS

- Tea room at Rhodes Memorial
- Groot Constantia has two restaurants: 021 794 5128, www.grootconstantia.co.za
- Uitsig has three restaurants: 021 794 6500, www.constantia-uitsig.com
- Buitenverwachting has two restaurants: 021 794 5190, www.buitenverwachting.com
- Steenberg has two restaurants: 021 713 2211, www. steenberg-vineyards.co.za
- Booking is advised; wine tastings are offered at all the above at a nominal charge

Leopard sculpture by Ivan Mitford-Barberton

1903, when it was called the Beach Hotel. Stand on the beach opposite the hotel, and on the rocks on the left-hand side is a bronze sculpture of a leopard, the work of sculptor Ivan Mitford-Barberton, who lived in Hout Bay. The last time a leopard was spotted on the mountains around here was in 1938.

From the hotel head up **Chapman's Peak Drive** ❹; stop at **East Fort** ❺. The well-maintained fort is down a pathway facing the Sentinel, a 300-metre sheer cliff that guards the entrance to Hout Bay Harbour. The cannons protected part of the bay and were matched by the cannons at West Fort, next to the fishing harbour. The buildings above the road are a blockhouse, barracks and cookhouse, used by the men defending the fort, which was built in 1796 by the British. Along the coastline to the right, some of the supports for the jetty of a manganese mine on the mountain are still visible.

Chapman's Peak Drive was the brainchild of Sir Frederick de Waal, the first administrator of the Cape Province. Opened in 1922, it is a great feat of engineering. The surveyors who planned the route were often safety-roped to prevent them falling down the precipitous cliffs. The pass was built by means of convict labour and took six years to complete. In recent years, more modern engineering

Rusted remains of an old jetty used for a now defunct manganese mine

techniques have been added because of severe rock falls. The cost of these improvements resulted in the drive being tolled. The drive is famed for its spectacular scenery; it is nine kilometres long with 114 bends – drive slowly! The name is believed to come from John Chapman, the first mate of a British ship, the *Consent*, who was dispatched in a boat to investigate the bay in 1607.

View from Chapman's Peak Drive with Slangkop Point Lighthouse in the distance

The route continues through Noordhoek to Ou Kaapseweg Extension and right into Kommetjie Road. On the right is Imhoff Farm with its craft centre, part of an early land grant that established farms to provide provisions for the ships using the VOC winter anchorage at Simon's Bay. After a fire in 1958, the complex was rebuilt. The road continues through the town of Kommetjie and on to Scarborough, where there is an unusual rock formation by the side of the road, known as **Camel Rock ❻**.

The feeding of baboons in Table Mountain National Park is forbidden.

SHAEN ADEY/IOA

Continue south to the entrance of the **Cape of Good Hope Nature Reserve ❼**, on the right. Started in 1938 as a nature reserve, this became part of the Table Mountain National Park in 2004. It has 40 kilometres of coastline and covers an area of 7 750 hectares. The reserve has a rich and varied flora and fauna, including indigenous fynbos, a natural shrubland or heathland vegetation occurring in a small area of the Western Cape. The area is also home to a variety of animals such as zebra, eland and other antelope, as well as small mammals. The Buffelsfontein Visitor Centre

Skaiffe's Barn (above); *padrão* at Cape Point (below)

is worth a visit. Across the road, Skaiffe's Barn dates from when there were a number of farms here. Further down on the right is the *padrão* (cross) erected in honour of Portuguese navigator Bartholomew Dias, who rounded the Cape in 1487 and continued to beyond Mossel Bay before returning to the Cape in 1488. There is a similar cross on the other coast of this nature reserve at Bordjiesdrift, commemorating Vasco da Gama's voyage to the Cape in 1497. There is a parking area at Cape Point from where a funicular runs to the top. Alternatively, take the steps up the hill to the lighthouse, where you can enjoy breathtaking views of the sea and coastline.

Once out of the reserve, turn right and continue to Miller's Point. The Hugo Family vault, on the corner of Valley Road, Murdock Valley, is a graveyard on land that was the family farm. Before entering Simon's Town, a quick visit to the penguins at **Boulders** ❽ is interesting. This African penguin colony is a major attraction.

Simon's Town is described in an earlier chapter (see page 92). It is the best place for a refreshment stop.

The Roman Rock Lighthouse, off the coast at **Simon's Town** ❾, is the only one built on a rock in South Africa. It took four years to construct, and opened in 1861.

At Glencairn, you can remain on the coast road through Fish Hoek and Muizenberg (see page 110) or turn left on to the

Glencairn Expressway (M6) to the Ou Kaapse Weg route past **Silvermine** ⑩. The VOC wanted to prospect for mineral resources in the Cape, and during Simon van der Stel's time, sink holes were dug. Small deposits of silver were struck in the area called Silvermine, which is signposted on Ou Kaapse Weg.

The quickest way to **Groot Constantia wine estate** ⑪ is along the M3, the Van der Stel Freeway; turn off at Ladies Mile/Bergvliet. Turn left and continue to Constantia Main Road (the more scenic route is along the M42 past Tokai Forest). Turn left; the estate is on the left. The Groot Constantia Manor House, which was virtually rebuilt after a fire in 1925, has a collection of early Cape furniture. The visitors' centre displays a history of slavery, and the wine cellar has a magnificent pediment by Anton Anreith. Since the time of Simon van der Stel, the cultivation of vines and wine making have made this area famous. There are six wine estates in the Constantia Valley where you can taste and purchase wines.

SILVERMINE

Centrally situated within the Table Mountain National Park, this plateau provides facilities for picnics, barbecues and walking amid spectacular scenery surrounded by abundant fynbos.

The area is divided into two parts by the Ou Kaapse Weg (which follows the migratory path of animals many years ago). Silvermine East is more rugged in terrain than the western side, but has the attraction of the waterfall, which is best seen in winter. In the western section, the reservoir was built in 1898 to supply the Kalk Bay and Muizenberg Municipality with water. There is a boardwalk around the dam, which is suitable for wheelchairs. Mountain biking is allowed in demarcated areas.

SHAEN ADEY/IOA

The African penguin colony at Boulders Beach is a major tourist attraction.

NIGEL DENNIS/IOA

Proteas in the Kirstenbosch National Botanical Garden (above); plaque commemorating the people of Protea Village (below)

From here, turn left and go up to Constantia Nek, where there is a cannon that was used to send signals to the Castle if there were enemy ships in False Bay or Hout Bay. Go along Rhodes Drive, which winds through avenues of chestnuts planted by Rhodes, to **Kirstenbosch National Botanical Garden ⑫**. At the top gate, turn right into Klaassens Drive, one kilometre along is a commemorative plaque denoting Van Riebeeck's hedge of wild almond trees, which delineated the boundary of the early Cape settlement.

Return to the main entrance and visit one of the most beautiful botanical gardens in the world. Set against the magnificent backdrop of Table Mountain, Kirstenbosch has mainly indigenous South African plants and has a particularly interesting glasshouse.

The gardens are believed to be named after J.F. Kirsten, a VOC official who farmed here. In 1895 Cecil John Rhodes purchased the land and presented it to the nation for the establishment of a botanical garden. In 1913 Harold Pearson became the first director. He is buried in the garden and his epitaph reads, 'All ye who seek his monument, look around'. The little stone church opposite the gardens is from 1866; Sophy Gray (Bishop Gray's wife – see page 128) designed the church for staff who worked on the Bishopscourt Estate. The current Chapel of the Good Shepherd was designed by the architect Kendall in 1904. A plaque commemorates the forced removal of the people of Protea Village under the Group Areas Act. The stone cottages opposite were built in 1924 as accommodation for girls who served a two year apprenticeship in the gardens. The scheme was terminated, as the demanding physical work in an isolated environment did not attract sufficient numbers and they were converted into workers' cottages.

Continue to Union Avenue (M3); turn left and go past Newlands Forest to **Rhodes Memorial ⑬**, from where there are magnificent views across the city. The memorial stands on what used to be Groote Schuur Estate, where Rhodes lived. Continue to Cape Town past Mostert's Mill and Groote Schuur Hospital.

TO THE GLORY OF GOD
Church of the Good Shepherd established circa 1884 in which the people of Protea Village worshipped until they were displaced by the Group Areas Act of 1950.
I give to you a new commandment: Love one another as I have loved you.

RHODES MEMORIAL

Opened in 1912 on 5 July (Rhodes's birthday), the memorial on the slopes of Devil's Peak was built of granite from the mountain excavated at Higgovale Quarry. It was designed by Sir Herbert Baker and J.M. Swan in the style of the Greek Temple at Paestum. The equestrian statue *Physical Energy* was sculpted by G.R. Watts (R.A.), and given as a gift to the people of South Africa. The eight bronze lions guarding the granite terraces are the work of Swan, who took his inspiration from the Egyptian Sphinxes. The bust in the central niche is also by Swan and the inscription above his head was written by Rudyard Kipling.

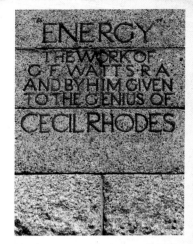

There are 49 steps up to the memorial, which represent the 49 years of Rhodes's life. The bench on which Rhodes often sat is behind a bush beneath the circular viewing terrace at the bottom of the memorial. The land to the left of the entrance gate, towards UCT, was the site of his private zoo. The memorial was paid for by public subscription – contributions could be made to the memorial account at any branch of Standard Bank. The main contributors were the mining houses.

A legacy Rhodes left to Cape Town was that he purchased large swathes of land below the mountain, thus preventing large-scale developments. These areas include Cecilia Forest, Kirstenbosch and the land on which UCT and Groote Schuur Hospital stand.

REFRESHMENTS
Take your own refreshments, including water

Al-Azhar Mosque

This painted floor tile in the District Six Museum commemorates life in the former suburb.

District Six

This area was originally known as Kanaldorp because of the canals that ran through it. After the emancipation of slaves in 1838, a number of them settled in this area. In 1867, when it was named one of the six municipal areas, parts of it were already overcrowded. There were also large houses and estates, such as Bloemhof and Zonnebloem. Hanover Street was named after the large house that German builder Herman Schutte erected. He named the new dwelling Hanover House, after the town in Germany. As the pressure on housing in the town grew, the neighbourhood expanded its borders. Double- and triple-storey buildings developed along Hanover and Caledon streets during the Anglo-Boer War. It grew into a cosmopolitan, mixed community with a number of Jewish shopkeepers trading in the district for many years. It has been described in *South Africa: A Modern History* (edited by Davenport and Saunders) as a 'vibrant, poor, colourful, gang-ridden community'.

In 1948 the defeat of Jan Smuts's United Party by D.F. Malan's National Party by a five-seat majority ushered in the policy of apartheid and the territorial, social and economic separation this entailed. The Group Areas Act, first tabled in 1950, and amended subsequently, brought about the policy of separate residential areas for different racial groups. In the Cape Peninsula, many thousands of mainly coloured people were forcibly removed from suburbs such as District Six and others, including Simon's Town, Kalk Bay, Tramway Road in Sea Point, Newlands Village, Mowbray, Claremont and Wynberg. They were moved to new townships established on the Cape Flats, and often separated from long-standing neighbours and friends. Businesses were also affected – shops, cinemas, hotels and bars no longer had customers as the areas emptied.

Despite objections and appeals, the whole of District Six was demolished and cleared, with the exception of a few schools, houses and places of worship. Many sound and important buildings were demolished despite urgent pleas to retain conservation-worthy nodes. It is estimated that nearly 60 000 people were forcibly removed from District Six.

Subsequent government plans to redevelop the area did not include

DRIVE KEY
1. St Mark's Anglican Church
2. Al-Azhar Mosque
3. Moravian Chapel
4. New Apostolic Church
5. Holy Cross Centre and Roman Catholic Church
6. Zonnebloem College
7. Chapel Street Primary School
8. St Philip's Anglican Church
9. St Philip's Mission Chapel
10. Zeenatul Islam Mosque

SHAEN ADEY/IOA

Original street
signs on display
in the District Six
Museum

public opinion. This oversight brought about the formation of protest groups and opposition to rebuilding the area as a whites-only suburb. As a result, protest groups declared a 'salted-earth' policy against the development of the area. In the early 1980s, the Nationalist government provided large sites totalling 25 hectares for the then Technikon for building new teaching facilities and accommodation along the renamed Keizersgracht, which followed the line of the old Hanover Street. The City Council offered an alternative site in Maitland for 10 rands in an attempt to keep the area clear for future development. The offer was refused by the Minister of Education. Around 60 streets were bulldozed out of existence.

In 2012 a District Six Redevelopment Process was started by the District Six Beneficiary Trust to build 100 homes along Chapel Street for ex-residents. Thus far, a few small isolated pockets of housing have been developed. But the rest of this once vibrant area is empty and desolate.

THE DRIVE

Start at the corner of Buitenkant and Darling streets. Drive up Darling Street and then into Keizersgracht. On the right-hand side is **St Mark's Anglican Church ❶**. The first chapel collapsed, and G.M. Alexander designed the current place of worship, which

St Mark's Anglican
Church, District Six

was completed in 1887, using Table Mountain sandstone. It was built as a thank-offering in the year of Queen Victoria's Golden Jubilee. St Mark's is an impressive building, despite being dominated by the large CPUT campus surrounding it. A commemorative tablet on the side of the church marks the demise of District Six.

Diagonally across the road is the **Al-Azhar Mosque ❷**, which was built circa 1900. This small mosque with its minaret can be found just off Keizersgracht.

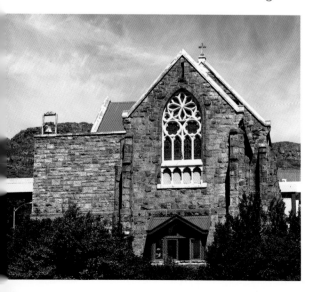

On Russel Road, off Keizersgracht, is the **Moravian Chapel** ❸, built on what was known as Moravian Hill, which is now part of the CPUT campus. Erected in 1886, the chapel has a porch with separate entrances for men and women. On the side of the building is the original parsonage, which has since been restored. The complex is once again being used for church services.

Moravian Church, Keizersgracht

Towards the Woodstock (eastern) end of Keizersgracht, on the left, is the **New Apostolic Church** ❹. A little further along, in Searle Street, is the **Holy Cross Centre** and **Roman Catholic Church** ❺. On the opposite side is the **Zonnebloem College** ❻ and Zonnebloem Estate in Cambridge Street. The land grant dates from 1707 and the main house from around 1800.

Turn left down Searle Street and go under Nelson Mandela Boulevard. Turn left into Chapel Street, which ran from Searle Street to Hanover Street, in the heart of District Six. The double-storey red-brick **Chapel Street Primary School** ❼ dates from 1912; some of the remaining simple terraced cottages are found in adjacent Francis and Osbourne streets. The lanes between the terraces (now gated up) were known as 'sanitary lanes' from where 'night soil' was collected in the days before sewerage was installed. **St Philip's Anglican Church** ❽, also in Chapel Street, was designed by Sir Herbert Baker in 1898. Chapel Street gets its name from the **St Philip's Mission Chapel** ❾, completed in 1885. It is now the site of an alternative theatre. Further along Chapel Street is the large **Zeenatul Islam Mosque** ❿, which was built in 1923 and has played a major part in the religious and cultural life of District Six.

There is a much quoted comment, attributed to a resident in 1966, that sums up the feeling of the former residents: 'You can take the people out of the heart of District Six, but you will never take District Six out of the heart of the people.'

It is through the determination of religious leaders and their congregants that the churches and mosques have survived in this area even though many of the congregations were forcibly dispersed across the Cape Flats.

The Saturday Neighbourgoods Market has a range of exciting crafts.

The Old Biscuit Mill

Woodstock

Steeped in history, this old suburb east of Cape Town was originally called Papendorp, after Pieter van Papendorp, a farmer who owned land between the Castle (see page 51) and Salt River. The name changed when the first Village Management Board in 1809 proposed the name New Brighton – after a local hotel. At a public meeting, a large group of fishermen who patronised the Woodstock Hotel outvoted the others and the neighbourhood acquired the name of the more popular inn.

Dom Francisco de Almeida, the Portuguese Viceroy of India, was killed on Woodstock Beach on 1 March 1510 during a skirmish with the Khoikhoi. He was returning to his homeland from India. This event played a role in Portugal's decision not to colonise the Cape.

The arrival of the railway in the early 1860s contributed to the development of the small suburb, and by 1881, it formed a separate municipality together with Salt River.

Woodstock is undergoing an urban renaissance, and a number of buildings have been restored or redeveloped, housing a range of creative enterprises from decor shops to art galleries to markets.

THE DRIVE

Start at Trafalgar Park, Searle Street. The **French Redoubt ❶** was built in 1781 by a French garrison stationed at the Cape. It formed part of a line of forts hastily constructed by the VOC, fearing an attack by the British as a result of events in Europe. The earth banks and stone entrance remain, as do a few cannons. The brick kiln-like chimney in the fort has been the focus of much speculation as to its purpose. It seems fairly clear now that it was a lime kiln. As you look from the Redoubt towards the mountain, the three British forts that were built after the first British occupation are the King's Blockhouse, high up on the slopes of Devil's Peak; Queen's Blockhouse, the next one down; and the remains of the Prince of Wales, the lowest. The British built these to strengthen their previous lines of defence.

The French Redoubt has now been fenced off for security reasons. However, a key to the gate can be obtained from the Trafalgar Park office on the corner of Victoria Road and Searle Street. Trafalgar Park contains a bandstand recalling the days when military bands played here.

At the junction of Victoria Road and Searle Street stood the old **toll gate ❷**. Introduced after the second British occupation, it was used to raise money for the building and maintenance of roads. A charge was made for horses and carts, ox wagons, and sheep and cattle going into the town. Today the bus depot and offices retain the name 'toll gate'.

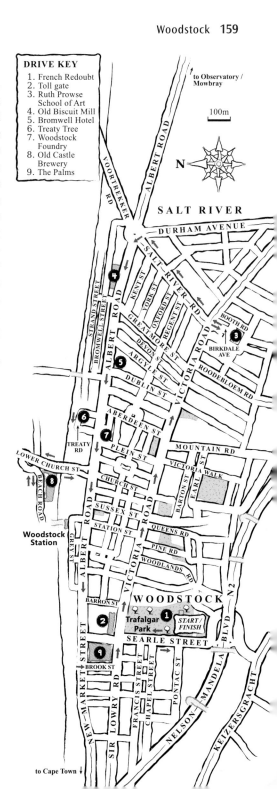

DRIVE KEY
1. French Redoubt
2. Toll gate
3. Ruth Prowse School of Art
4. Old Biscuit Mill
5. Bromwell Hotel
6. Treaty Tree
7. Woodstock Foundry
8. Old Castle Brewery
9. The Palms

The former Bromwell Hotel, now a boutique mall (above); Ruth Prowse School of Art (below)

Go south-east along Victoria Road; at the start of Salt River, Birkdale Avenue is on the right. Look for the sign to the **Ruth Prowse School of Art** ❸. The Georgian-style building, which can be seen from Victoria Road, has been beautifully restored and is used as an art college. The land was first granted in 1661, and this is one of the oldest houses in the area.

From Birkdale, turn left into Victoria Road and then right into Salt River Road. At the circle, turn left into Albert Road. On the right is the **Old Biscuit Mill** ❹, Nos. 373–389 Albert Road. This was Pyotts Biscuit Factory and the Standard Flour Mill. The complex has been redeveloped, maintaining some of the old features. It has an eclectic mixture of shops and restaurants, and

on Saturdays the Neighbourgoods Market draws large crowds. A little further on the left is the **Bromwell** ❺; it was formerly an Ohlsson's Brewery hotel. There is now a restaurant-cum-bakery downstairs and a display of designer products upstairs.

Further on, on the right, is Treaty Road. Turn into this road, and around the corner stands a milkwood tree in a small park. A small cottage (now demolished) used to stand here and this is where the treaty was signed after the Battle of Blaauwberg (see page 181). On 10 January 1806, Lieutenant Colonel Baron von Prophalov came from the Castle to sign the document, it is said under the shade of the tree known as the **Treaty Tree** ❻.

Return to Albert Road. Continue towards Cape Town until you reach No. 105, the **Woodstock Foundry** ❼, on the corner of Plein Street. This was the site of the Montpelier Bar, which belonged to Ohlsson's Brewery.

From Albert Road, turn right at Church Street, go over the railway bridge, and then turn left into Beach Road. The **old Castle Brewery** ❽ was built by Johannesburg-based South African Breweries during the Anglo-Boer War of 1899–1902. Designed by American architect H. Steinmann, it was built in the form of a castle as an advertisement for the product. The brewing equipment was imported from the USA. The brewery closed down in 1956 when it merged with Ohlsson's Brewery. The complex has been renovated and is used as offices and studios. The nine-metre spire has been replaced. To get the best view of this unusual building, walk back to the bridge. It is hard today to comprehend that the sea once came up to the beach here. The land was reclaimed when Cape Town Harbour was expanded in the 1940s.

Turn left up Brook Street – the large design and decor complex called **The Palms** ❾, on Sir Lowry Road, was the Baumann Biscuit Factory. The centre retains some of the fabric of the original building.

From here, veer left into Victoria Road; Searle Street is close by on the right.

The Treaty Tree (above); the chimney at the Old Biscuit Mill (below), originally part of the Pyotts Biscuit Factory

USEFUL INFORMATION

University of Cape Town
021 650 9111
www.uct.ac.za

REFRESHMENTS

Wide variety of cafés, takeaways and pubs on Main Road

University of Cape Town

Rondebosch

Immediately after World War II the suburb of Rondebosch was very different from what it is today. Milk was delivered from Whitfields Dairy Farm in Klipfontein Road, and bread came by horse and cart from Cole's Bakery in Observatory.

A memorial urn on the university's Upper Campus

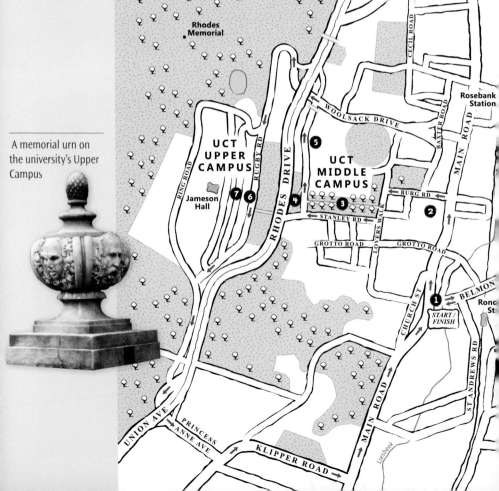

There was a small group of village shops on Main Road. The grocer, Mrs Scholnick, knew everybody by name and their particular requirements. The baker, Mr Keown, made birthday cakes in the shapes of rugby balls and cricket bats, which he displayed in his window. Hessen Brothers was a large grocery and hardware merchants on Main Road, which made deliveries by horse-drawn wagons, and had stables at the back of the premises. They bought a second-hand army truck for deliveries. After a couple of weeks it broke down, and urban legend has it that it was towed back by the horses.

Modern-day Rondebosch is a popular residential suburb and a busy student centre, heavily influenced by its proximity to the University of Cape Town.

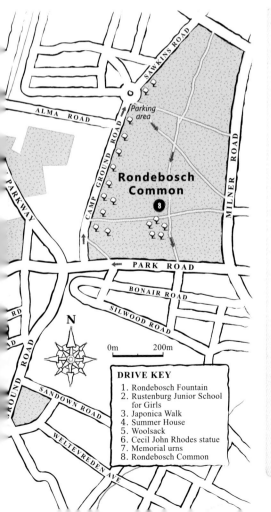

DRIVE KEY
1. Rondebosch Fountain
2. Rustenburg Junior School
   for Girls
3. Japonica Walk
4. Summer House
5. Woolsack
6. Cecil John Rhodes statue
7. Memorial urns
8. Rondebosch Common

SIR HERBERT BAKER

Born in England in 1862, architect Herbert Baker arrived in South Africa in 1892. In 1893 he started work on remodelling Groote Schuur for Rhodes in the Cape Dutch style, for which he became famous. He designed houses, churches and commercial buildings in the Cape before moving to Johannesburg in 1902. Baker also designed the Union Buildings in Pretoria in 1913. He then left South Africa to work with Sir Edward Lutyens in New Delhi. He left behind partnerships in Cape Town, Johannesburg and Bloemfontein that bore his name until the 1920s. Baker also designed South Africa House and the Bank of England in London.

Trovato House in Wynberg was designed by Herbert Baker and completed in 1902 (see Wynberg map on page 121).

THE DRIVE

This could also be undertaken as an active walk, but there are a lot of steps up to the university and a slope up to Middle Campus. This chapter should be read in conjunction with the Liesbeek Trail (page 130).

Start at the **Rondebosch Fountain** ❶, on the corner of Main and Belmont roads, then turn right along Main Road. Shortly after Grotto Road on the left is **Rustenburg Junior School for Girls** ❷. A house was built on this site in 1657; later it was rebuilt and became the country residence of the governor. The second storey was added in 1780. Rustenburg Junior occupies this old building, which formed the axis of a formal landscape leading to the governor's summer house. In 1795, after the Battle of Muizenberg (see page 114), the articles of capitulation were signed in the house and it became British property. The four large Ionic columns were added in the early nineteenth century. The house was badly damaged by fire in the mid-1850s. On the left of the main building are two guardhouses, which flank today's school hall. It is thought they were designed by Louis Thibault.

Turn left into Burg Road and then left into Lovers Walk. On the right, the pathway up **Japonica Walk** ❸ leads to the **Summer House** ❹, which was built in 1760. Drive up Stanley Road and turn right into UCT's Middle Campus. Japonica Walk was planted when Cecil John Rhodes owned the property; it followed the line of an avenue of trees that led to the Summer House. It was restored by Herbert Baker and there are good views across the Cape Flats from the roof balcony. (If you are walking, take the tunnel under Rhodes Drive next to the Summer House.) Drive along the road, and on the right is **Woolsack** ❺, designed by Herbert Baker in the Cape Dutch Revival style and built in 1900. Rhodes's instruction to the architect was to design a 'cottage in the woods for poets and artists'. English writer Rudyard Kipling was a frequent guest here.

Turn left up Woolsack Drive onto UCT Upper Campus and then left onto Rugby Road next to the fields. The seated **statue of Cecil John Rhodes** ❻ was sculpted by Marion Walgate. Up on Chancellor's Walk, in front of Jammie Steps,

Japonica Walk, leading to the Summer House on the UCT Middle Campus which lead up to Jameson Hall, are four **memorial urns** ❼. These flank the steps and were designed by Grace Wheatley. The urns commemorate Sir Carruthers Beattie (first vice chancellor of UCT); Professor C.E. Lewis (classics); Professor Lawrence Crawford (pure maths); and Professor Alexander Brown (applied maths). There are heritage maps in the middle and upper campuses displaying items of historical interest.

From Rugby Road, turn left onto the one-way road to Princess Anne Avenue and then left into Klipper Road. At the intersection with Main Road, turn left. When you reach the fountain, turn right to go down Belmont Road, across Liesbeek Parkway, and left into Camp Ground Road. **Rondebosch Common** ❽ on the right-hand side was first used in 1805, when General Janssens's Batavian Force camped out here while they were preparing for the British attack during the Battle of Blaauwberg. In the cold winter a number died of dysentery, including Janssens's 17-year-old son. After the British victory, the common was used for military purposes. There is a parking area opposite the traffic circle; follow any of the paths across the common towards the circle of trees near Park Road. In 1855 the rector of St Paul's Church was given permission to graze cattle on the common with the proviso that the public were allowed access. At the same time, the Wesleyan and Muslim communities were granted burial grounds – the pine trees border these grounds. In 1853 civil engineer Andrew Bain (who built Bain's Kloof pass) sank a shaft in search of coal which, thankfully, he did not find.

The common used to be larger than it is today. It is a pleasant open space in Cape Town's suburban sprawl. In spring more than 240 species of wild flowers grow here.

Return along Camp Ground Road (whose name is a reminder of its military heritage) and Belmont Road to the starting point.

Statue of Cecil John Rhodes on the UCT Upper Campus
SHAEN ADEY/IOA

Former burial ground, surrounded by pine trees, on Rondebosch Common

DISTANCE
± 60 km

USEFUL INFORMATION

Constantia Wine Route
021 794 5011
www.constantiawineroute.
co.za

Groot Constantia Iziko Museum
admission charge;
children under 16, free
021 795 5140

REFRESHMENTS

■ Alphen Boutique Hotel:
021 794 5011
■ The Cellars-Hohenort:
021 794 2137
■ Greens Restaurant (with outside terrace), High Constantia Shopping Centre: 021 794 7843,
www.greensrestaurant.co.za
■ Jonkershuis (Groot Constantia):
021 794 6255; www. jonkershuisconstantia.co.za
■ Simon's at Groot Constantia: 021 794 1143,
www.simons.co.za

Klein Constantia wine estate

Constantia & Tokai

The beautiful Constantia Valley to the south of Cape Town has the closest vineyards and wine farms to the city. Favoured in times past by the Khoikhoi, who seasonally grazed their cattle and sheep here, this area retains a semi-rural character. A few wine estates, with their old Dutch homesteads, and two flower farms remind us of the area's rich agricultural heritage.

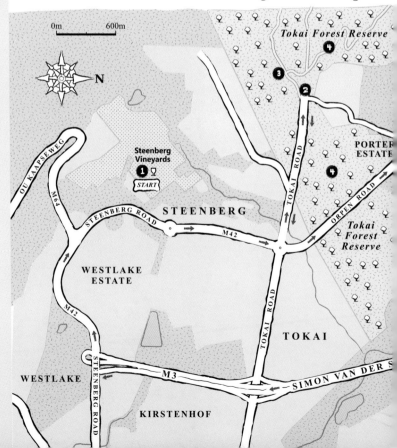

Groot Constantia is one of South Africa's oldest wine estates and among the best known. The manor house is a cultural-history museum with a good collection relating to the area's past, including slavery. There are a number of theories as to how the farm, and subsequently the area, was named Constantia. The most likely explanation is that it was named after the daughter of Commissioner Van Goens, a VOC official who supported Simon van der Stel's land grant.

Egyptian geese are often seen in the Constantia Valley.

It is generally agreed that Tokai is named after a range of mountains in a wine-growing area of Hungary known for its sweet wines.

This drive starts at the southern end of the valley and winds its way to the lovely Alphen Hotel with its historic buildings. Also included is a brief history of the Constantia Cemetery to illustrate how even a graveyard can make local history come alive.

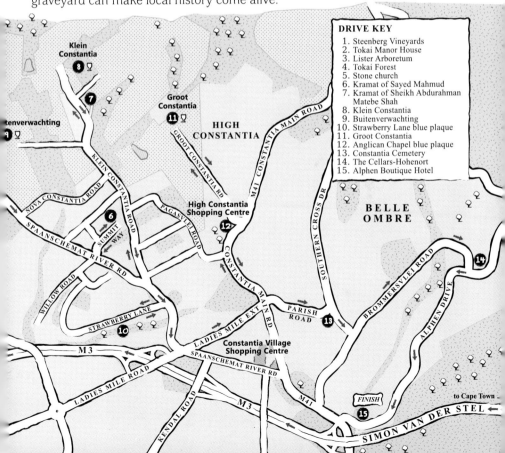

DRIVE KEY

1. Steenberg Vineyards
2. Tokai Manor House
3. Lister Arboretum
4. Tokai Forest
5. Stone church
6. Kramat of Sayed Mahmud
7. Kramat of Sheikh Abdurahman Matebe Shah
8. Klein Constantia
9. Buitenverwachting
10. Strawberry Lane blue plaque
11. Groot Constantia
12. Anglican Chapel blue plaque
13. Constantia Cemetery
14. The Cellars-Hohenort
15. Alphen Boutique Hotel

THE DRIVE

Take the M3 south from Cape Town to its end; turn right. Follow the M42 until you reach **Steenberg Vineyards** ❶ on the left.

The first settler in this valley was an amazing woman called Catharina Ustings, who came from Lübeck, on the Baltic coast of Germany. A 22-year-old widow, she braved the long sea voyage and arrived at the Cape in 1662. Her second husband was Hans Ras, a free burgher with a farm on the Liesbeek River; he was killed by a lion. Her third husband was killed in a fight with a Khoikhoi. Her fourth husband was trampled to death by an elephant. Her fifth husband, Mattys Michelse, was also a free burgher. By this time, she realised that marriage was not a source of security for her so she decided to invest in property. In 1682 she persuaded Simon van der Stel to lease her land for a farm at Steenberg (Stone Mountain). She named the farm Swaaneweide – the feeding place of the swans, after a town in Germany. In 1688 a legal title deed was granted. Baron van Rheede, commissioner of the VOC, noted in his diary that he had a healthy meal of radishes, cabbage and freshly baked bread at Catharina's homestead. His description of the lady of the house was that she rode bareback 'like an Indian' and her children resembled 'Brazilian cannibals'.

Steenberg, in Tokai, is one of the oldest farms in the Cape Peninsula.

The farm was renamed Steenberg and the main house was built around 1765. Don't be misled by the date on the gable, which refers to the lease date. It has the only holbol gable remaining in the Cape Peninsula. The house is now part of the Steenberg Hotel complex.

From Steenberg, turn left onto the M42 and left up Tokai Road. **Tokai Manor House** ❷ is a handsome building with a commanding view over the valley from its high front stoep (veranda). It was built to the design of Louis Thibault in 1795–1796. One New Year's Eve in the early nineteenth century, the son of the owner rode his white horse up the flight of steps onto the balcony and around the guests seated at the dinner table. As he rode down the other staircase, his horse tripped and he was killed. It is claimed that on New Year's Eve the sound of horse's hooves can be heard. The house is now part of the Table Mountain National Park and it is hoped that the public will be able to gain access to the building.

Further along the road is the **Lister Arboretum** ❸, initiated in 1885 by Joseph Storr Lister, the chief conservator of forests for the Cape Colony. He planted some 150 species of trees from wam temperate countries, including several magnificent American redwoods.

Tokai Forest ❹ has walking and cycle paths, and a picnic/braai (barbecue) area.

The kramat of Sayed Mahmud, who was banished to Constantia in the late 1660s, is on Summit Way in Constantia.

Go down Tokai Road and turn left onto the M42 towards Cape Town. There is a small **stone church** ❺ built on the grounds of the former William Porter Reformatory for boys in Tokai. Some claim Sir Herbert Baker had a hand in its design.

Summit Way is on the left. The kramat of **Sayed Mahmud** ❻ is on Islam Hill. He was a spiritual and religious leader of the Malaccan Empire, captured and exiled by the VOC from Sumatra in 1668. He was banished to the forest of Constantia to keep him away from the growing slave population in the Cape.

Continue along the M42 (Spaanschemat River Road) and make a sharp left turn up Klein Constantia Road. At the circle at the top a narrow road leads to the kramat of **Sheikh Abdurahman Matebe Shah** ❼, a Malaccan sultan. A new structure was designed by architect Gawie Fagan to house the grave. From the circle, a driveway leads to **Klein Constantia wine estate** ❽. Although the estate has modern wine-tasting facilities, the stately homestead is from 1790. Also along Klein Constantia Road is the turn-off to **Buitenverwachting wine estate** ❾. Its elegant homestead is dated 1796.

This pretty stone church on Orpen Road (M42) is on the grounds of the present-day Porter Estate in Tokai.

Back on the M42, on the right, is **Strawberry Lane** ❿, thus named because a community of mainly tenant farmers used to

SHAEN ADEY/IOA

The manor house at Buitenverwachting was built in 1796.

grow strawberries and flowers here. Under the Group Areas Act, they were forcibly removed. A Simon van der Stel Foundation **blue plaque** has been erected in memory of this group of former residents.

Turn right onto the M42 again, and left into Ladies Mile Extension. Ladies Mile is named after the widow Colyn who, in the nineteenth century, fell out with a farmer about the right to ride her horse on a bridle path. She lost her case in the Wynberg Magistrates' Court, but appealed to the King in Council in London, where she won. The locals named this road after her victory.

A commemoration plaque in Strawberry Lane

Turn left at the traffic lights into Constantia Main Road and left into Groot Constantia Road. The best known of the historic homesteads in the peninsula is **Groot Constantia ⑪**, at the end of this road. Simon van der Stel was appointed commander of the Cape in 1679. Van der Stel displayed an interest in the new country unequalled by any of his predecessors. For example, in 1680 he founded the town of Stellenbosch and granted farms in the Drakenstein Valley; and he prospected for copper in Namaqualand. He also supported the Huguenot settlers in 1688, started a land registry and encouraged education. In 1685, in recognition of his services to the VOC and to develop the Cape's agricultural potential, he was given a large grant of 762 hectares of land in the valley that extended from Wynberg Hill to where Bergvliet is today. He built an 18-room, double-storey U-shaped homestead on the site of the current Groot Constantia. He retired in 1699 and ran his huge farm with enthusiasm. He experimented with seeds and plants brought to him by sea captains, who received a gift of Constantia wine in

Groot Constantia Manor House

SHAEN ADEY/IOA

return. The farm was sold in 1714, two years after his death, and divided into three portions – Groot Constantia, with the homestead, Klein Constantia and Bergvliet. After the property had changed ownership a number of times, Hendrik Cloete purchased it in 1778 and made many alterations. He built the wine cellar, which has a magnificent Ganymede pediment sculpture by Anton Anreith, dated 1791.

In 1885 the government acquired the property for use as an experimental wine farm and a training centre for viticulture. The homestead was severely damaged by fire in 1925, after which it was substantially restyled and rebuilt by architect F.K. Kendall. The Jonkershuis, now a restaurant, and the stables, now a visitors' centre, were untouched by the fire. An avenue of trees leads to the old exterior bath. As well as the exhibits in the main house, there is also an exhibition on wine making. Wine tasting and cellar tours are available. There are two restaurants, which provide picnic lunches on request.

From the Constantia wine estate, turn right into Constantia Main Road. The blue plaque under the trees near the High Constantia Shopping Centre marks the site of the first **Anglican Chapel** ⑫ and school in the Constantia Valley. Turn left at Parish Road, and near the intersection with Southern Cross Drive, on the right, is the **Constantia Cemetery** ⑬ (see page 173).

Turn right into Southern Cross Drive and left into Brommersvlei Road. Near the top of the road is **The Cellars-Hohenort hotel** ⑭, which has beautiful gardens. The historic house, Hohenort, is now part of the hotel. From here, turn right into Alphen Drive and continue to the intersection with the M41. On the right find the attractive double-storey **Alphen Hotel** ⑮, a former manor house that was built in about 1765. This elegant complex has buildings on three sides, including the original cellars and stables. Today it operates as a hotel, restaurant and outdoor café.

After your visit, make your way back to Constantia Main Road in order to access the M3.

The elegant Alphen Hotel in Constantia is a heritage site.

CONSTANTIA CEMETERY

Established on 16 June 1886, the cemetery lay between Belle Ombre and Rust en Vrede farms. It is now under the control of the City of Cape Town. The surrounding farms in 1880 were:

- **Witteboomen** – Constantia Main Road
- **Nieuw Constantia** – now Silverhurst
- **Belle Ombre** – on the mountain side of Southern Cross Drive
- **Claasenbosch** – Brommersvlei Road
- **Rust en Vrede** – Brommersvlei Road
- **Alphen** – which ran across the sports fields and the freeway of today.

The Rathfelder family grave

The first three rows of graves nearest Parish Road contain the remains of some of the pioneers of Constantia. In 1857 William George Gilmour bought New Constantia Farm. Born in Edinburgh, Gilmour came to the Cape when he was 14, bought a horse and cart, and became a *smous* (pedlar), touring Namaqualand and later the Transvaal. He made his fortune, and is said to have paid for the farm with gold sovereigns he had saved. His Irish wife renamed the farm Silverhurst, after the colour of the leaves of the silver trees growing on the estate. Gilmour's son Hugh John inherited the estate, and he and his family are buried in the cemetery.

Belle Ombre Farm was originally called Goedgeloof. Dr James Hutchinson, a surgeon who had practised in India, bought the farm and changed the name to Belle Ombre (meaning beautiful shade). He died in 1870. An obelisk originally erected next to his grave now stands in the front garden of a house at 4 Provence Avenue. The grave was removed and he was reburied in the Constantia Cemetery. Johannes Rathfelder, of German extraction, purchased Belle Ombre in 1872. Members of his family ran Rathfelder's Inn on Main Road, Diep River, a successful and popular inn halfway on the road between Cape Town and Simon's Town. Rathfelder left the farm to his son Otto in 1902. His daughter married a Schuddingh and her family is buried here as well.

Claasenbosch (now spelt with a 'K') was bought by Arnold Wilhelm Spilhaus in September 1906. He demolished the old house and built a large house with German-style square gables. His forefathers came from Tiefenort, which means 'low place' in German. Spilhaus named his Constantia house on the hillside overlooking the valley Hohenort, meaning 'high place'. It is now part of The Cellars-Hohenort hotel. Spilhaus was 101 when he died.

Frederick Bullen-Moore was the first rector of Christ Church Constantia, from 1866 to 1913. His gravestone and those of his family are in the cemetery. He lived in Wynberg and commuted to Constantia in his horse and trap.

There is a line of military graves in the centre of Constantia Cemetery. The men buried here were medical orderlies of the Royal Army Medical Corps who fell victim to the 1903 typhoid epidemic that swept through the demobilisation camp set up in Wynberg after the Anglo-Boer War. The white gravestones were given by family or colleagues; the black ones were provided by the War Graves Commission.

The cemetery contains the graves of a large group of Constantia residents – some of the poorer could not afford headstones. They would have had wooden or metal crosses, which have disappeared over the years.

Rondevlei marshland

Rondevlei Nature Reserve

Four hundred years ago, there were dozens of vleis (marshlands) across the sandy Cape Flats. Some of the vleis were home to hippos. When the Europeans came in the seventeenth century, armed with guns, the hippo population was annihilated within 50 years. The meat was popular, as was venison from buck, and was used to supply ships, which were in need of fresh meat.

The Rondevlei Nature Reserve lies just off the M5 near the neighbourhood of Grassy Park. Founded in 1952 by the Divisional Council of the Cape and run by the City of Cape Town, its 290 hectares provide an important natural environment in the middle of the peninsula. It contains a wide range of indigenous

DISTANCE FROM M5
± 9 km

DISTANCE FROM CITY CENTRE
± 32 km

USEFUL INFORMATION
Imvubu Nature Tours
021 706 0842
www.imvubu.co.za

Rondevlei
Nature Reserve
admission charge;
charge for fishing permits;
open daily, except
Christmas day
021 706 2404
www.capetown.gov.za/
environment

REFRESHMENTS
Take your own refreshments

Rondevlei Nature
Reserve protects
a small population
of hippos.

NIGEL DENNIS/IOA

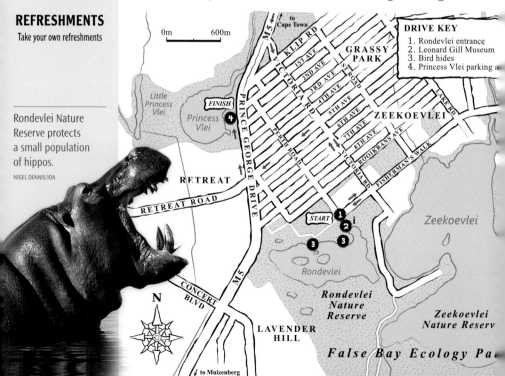

0m   600m

to
Cape Town

DRIVE KEY
1. Rondevlei entrance
2. Leonard Gill Museum
3. Bird hides
4. Princess Vlei parking a

KLIP RD
1ST AVE
2ND AVE
3RD AVE
4TH AVE
5TH AVE
6TH AVE
7TH AVE
8TH AVE

GRASSY PARK

ZEEKOEVLEI

Little Princess Vlei

FINISH

Princess Vlei

PRINCE GEORGE DRIVE

PERTH ROAD

ROOIKRANS AVE

FISHERMAN'S WALK

LAKE RD

RETREAT

RETREAT ROAD

START

i

Zeekoevlei

CONCERT BLVD

M5

Rondevlei

Rondevlei Nature Reserve

Zeekoevlei Nature Reserv

N

LAVENDER HILL

False Bay Ecology Pa

to Muizenberg

SHAEN ADEY/IOA

plant species and is home to a number of mammals. A small group of hippos has been reintroduced, and there are Cape grysbok, porcupines, large spotted genets and Cape clawless otters, to name a few. The reserve is also a haven for birds, particularly waterbirds. Since 1952, over 240 bird species have been recorded here.

Pelicans are one of the many bird species that inhabit Rondevlei Nature Reserve.

The **reserve entrance** ❶, off Fisherman's Walk, is clearly marked. The **Leonard Gill Museum** ❷ has a display of birds and animals found in the reserve, a small reptile area and an aquarium. There are also two observation towers and a number of **hides** ❸ overlooking the water. There is a picnic area and a toilet block nearby. A garden nursery sells plants suitable for wetlands, lowlands and coastal areas.

A private tour company (Imvubu Nature Tours) offers overnight stays on an island bush camp, as well as boat trips and guided walks. There is also a private function area.

Zeekoevlei is nearby. In 1656 Jan van Riebeeck visited the area and found it to be 'full of hippopotami'. Today it is a residential area with private yacht and rowing clubs.

Princess Vlei

Princess Vlei ❹, named after a Khoikhoi princess who visited the Elephant Eye Cave above Tokai Forest, is a couple of kilometres north of the M5. There is a parking area overlooking the water. The vlei is the focus of an environmental regeneration project called 'Dressing the Princess'.

USEFUL INFORMATION

Cape Tourist Guide Association
www.ctga.org.za

Cape Town Tourism
for information on tours with registered tour guides or companies
021 487 6800
www.capetown.travel

REFRESHMENTS

Take your own refreshments

Crafts made in Philippi
on the Cape Flats

Lutheran Church, Philippi

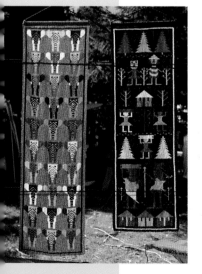

Cape Flats

Tens of thousands of years ago, the area between Table Mountain and the Boland Mountains was under shallow seawater. The Cape Flats, as this area is known, was once a marine environment, and is distinguished by its white sandy soil. This sandy isthmus was a major obstacle in obtaining access to the interior in the early days of the Cape Colony. The first route to the north followed the line of the Tygerberg Hills and then branched to Stellenbosch and Somerset West, and further afield.

In the 1920s the first tarred road across the sandy Cape Flats, stretching from Athlone to Somerset West, was opened, and even then sand storms closed it from time to time.

Between 1858 and 1883, groups of German settlers arrived to farm on the Cape Flats. They were blissfully unaware of the problems and challenges that faced them. They were based in Philippi and many of their descendants continue to farm produce there today. The Lutheran Church at Philippi stands as a tribute to this hardy group of pioneers.

Athlone, Crawford and Lansdowne were early housing suburbs that depended on the Cape Flats railway line for their existence before a connecting road system was developed.

In 1948 the defeat of Smuts's United Party by D.F. Malan's National Party ushered in apartheid. The implementation of the Group Areas Act of 1950 forced many thousands of people to move. It is estimated that 60 000 people were forced to move from District Six alone (see page 154). The government provided subeconomic housing across the Cape Flats; and suburbs such as Manenberg and Bonteheuwel were developed. Rylands was allocated to the Indian community. Today Mitchell's Plain and its surrounding suburbs have a population of close to 2 million people.

The first township for black Africans was Langa, meaning the sun, followed by Nyanga (the moon) and Gugulethu (our pride). The newest and largest township is Khayelitsha, meaning new home, which is 40 kilometres from the city and has a population of over 1 million.

The best way to experience the Cape Flats and the vibrant lifestyle of this area is to take a guided tour. Most tours include visits to memorials and sites where anti-apartheid protests took place. They also take visitors to a number of craft centres where curios as well as traditional beadwork can be viewed and purchased. In Khayelitsha a visit to Lookout Hill provides a 360-degree view from the top of the dunes.

This plaque in Philippi honours the arrival of the first German settlers on the Cape Flats (above). The Trojan Horse memorial in Athlone recalls the 'struggle era' killing of three people in 1985 by security police disguised as railway employees (below).

View from Durbanville Hills

USEFUL INFORMATION

Blaauwberg Conservation Area
021 554 0957
www.bca.org.za

Durbanville Rose Garden
021 976 4497

Durbanville Wine Route
www.durbanvillewine.co.za

Rust en Vrede Cultural Centre
021 976 4691
www.rust-en-vrede.com

South African Air Force Museum, Ysterplaat
021 508 6526
www.saairforce.co.za/the-airforce/history/saaf-museum/locations/ysterplaat

REFRESHMENTS

■ Durbanville Hills wine estate (wine tasting and restaurant with superb views of Table Mountain): 021 558 1300; www.durbanvillehills.co.za
■ Nitida (wine tasting and restaurants): 021 976 1467, www.nitida.co.za
■ Ons Huisie Restaurant, Bloubergstrand: 021 554 1553

The wooden bridge across the Milnerton lagoon to Woodbridge Island was built in 1901 by the Royal Engineers.

Blouberg & Durbanville

This drive offers the opportunity to walk on the beaches at Milnerton and Bloubergstrand. Swimming is only advised at Milnerton Beach and Big Bay when life guards are on duty. Blouberg means blue mountain, a reference to the bluish colour of Blouberg Hill when seen from the sea or across the bay from the city.

The Air Force Museum en route will appeal to aviation buffs. The rolling hills on the way to Durbanville contain vineyards that thrive on the cooler sea breezes wafting from the ocean; some offer wine tasting and have restaurants.

Durbanville was originally called Pampoenkraal, the name of a local farm. It was renamed D'Urban in 1836 in honour of Sir Benjamin D'Urban, governor of the Cape from 1834 to 1838. In 1886 it was given its present name to avoid confusion with the town in Natal. Durbanville's restored windmill, Onze Molen, reminds us that there were many similar wind-powered mills around the Cape in the nineteenth century.

THE DRIVE

Coming from Cape Town on the N1, take the Koeberg Road turn-off to Brooklyn. From Koeberg Road, turn right into Piet Grobler Street. The **South African Air Force Museum** ❶ at Ysterplaat Aerodrome provides interesting displays with active exhibits on the history of aviation in South Africa.

Continue along Koeberg Road towards Milnerton, turn left into Loxton Street and go over the bridge to Woodbridge Island. The **wooden bridge** ❷, to the right, across the lagoon was built by the Royal Engineers in 1901 using imported jarrah wood. The British forces in the Cape were afraid of an attack from the sea by a country or group supporting the Boer forces during the Anglo-Boer War and mounted a gun emplacement overlooking the beach.

By the side of Marine Drive is a **plaque** ❸ commemorating the opening of the railway line on 26 December 1903 between Cape Town and Milnerton. The railway famously transported

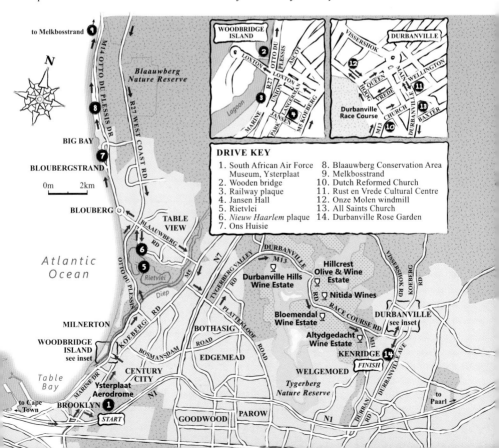

DRIVE KEY

1. South African Air Force Museum, Ysterplaat
2. Wooden bridge
3. Railway plaque
4. Jansen Hall
5. Rietvlei
6. *Nieuw Haarlem* plaque
7. Ons Huisie
8. Blaauwberg Conservation Area
9. Melkbosstrand
10. Dutch Reformed Church
11. Rust en Vrede Cultural Centre
12. Onze Molen windmill
13. All Saints Church
14. Durbanville Rose Garden

The Southern African Foundation for the Conservation of Coastal Birds (SANCCOB), a seabird sanctuary, is near the site where shipwreck survivors set up camp in 1647.

SHAEN ADEY/IOA

passengers to Milnerton Racecourse. The racecourse is no longer used for races, but a portion of it still contains stables and horse-training facilities.

Jansen Hall ❹, on the corner of Jansen and Park roads, was built in 1904 as a tea room. It is an unusual construction within a timber framework. It has seen use as a casino, dance hall and concert venue.

Continue on Marine Drive past **Rietvlei** ❺. Turn right into Blaauwberg Road and right again into Pentz Drive. Next to the SANCCOB seabird sanctuary at No. 22, on the right-hand side, is a small parking area and on the wall of the house on the left is a **plaque** ❻ commemorating the site where the survivors from the VOC ship *Nieuw Haarlem*, wrecked in Table Bay in 1647, set up their camp. Using fresh water from the spring nearby, they survived for nearly a year before they were collected by the fleet returning from the East Indies. This became a VOC outpost for a number of years. It is also the site where General Janssens (commander of the Batavian forces in the Cape) marshalled his forces before the Battle of Blaauwberg.

At Blaauwberg Road turn left and cross the West Coast Road to Otto du Plessis Drive, which skirts the beach. Follow the signs on the left to **Ons Huisie** ❼, on Stadler Road. This was a fisherman's cottage, the only remaining one in the area before it was transformed into an eatery. Return to Otto du Plessis Drive, and continue in the same direction. The **Blaauwberg Conservation Area** ❽ is based at Eerstesteen, on the left. It contains an information centre, which documents the types of fynbos found in the area.

The suburb of **Melkbosstrand** ❾ has a long sandy beach, which the British forces chose as a landing place in 1806 before the Battle of Blaauwberg. Turn left into 6th Avenue and continue to the parking area on the beach front.

France and England had extensive interests in the East Indies, and the Cape was a crucial link on the sea route to the East. In 1806 France and England were at war, and the Cape was under the control of the Batavian Republic (Holland). The Dutch East India Company was bankrupt after the first British occupation of the Cape (1795–1802). Under the Treaty of Amiens, the Cape was then handed back to the French-allied revolutionary Batavian Republic, which had taken power in the Netherlands and expelled the Prince of Orange.

On 4 January 1806, a British fleet of 63 ships and nearly 7 000 troops anchored between Robben Island and Blouberg. Strong winds and heavy seas prevented a landing. General Janssens brought his smaller force of 2 000 men to Rietvlei. This consisted of small groups, including German and Austrian mercenaries, Batavian troops, French marines, a Javan artillery corps, burgher commandos and a Khoisan regiment. The British troops began landing at Losperd's Bay (now Melkbosstrand) on 6 January. The battle commenced on 8 January; Janssens's troops straddled the wagon trail to Cape Town. The conflict was short and furious, with the battle taking place on the plains on the eastern side of Blouberg Hill. On the Batavian front, confusion reigned and the mercenaries fled. Some retreated to Rietvlei. Janssens withdrew his burgher units to the Hottentots-Holland Mountains. Lieutenant Colonel Baron von Prophalov, the acting Batavian commander, capitulated and signed the surrender treaty in Woodstock on 10 January (see page 161).

SHAEN ADEY/IOA

The old slave bell at Altydgedacht wine estate on the Durbanville Wine Route (above); Durbanville's Dutch Reformed Church, which dates from 1890 (below)

From the beach, turn left into Melkbosstrand Road and turn right onto the R27 (West Coast Road) towards Cape Town. Turn left at Blaauwberg Road, continue to Koeberg Road, turn right and then left into Plattekloof Road (M14). Cross the N7 and turn left onto the M13 (Tygerberg Valley Road), which takes you to the Durbanville Hills and the suburb of Durbanville. The Durbanville Wine Route has a number of wine estates that you may wish to visit.

In Durbanville, go down Church Street; on the right is the **Dutch Reformed Church** ⑩. The original church was built in 1825. The present building was designed by architect Charles Freeman in 1890 and has an interesting graveyard.

Continue along Church Street and turn left into Main Road and right into Wellington Road. On the right is the attractive **Rust en Vrede Cultural Centre** ⑪, with an art gallery and clay museum. Said to be

The interior of All Saints Church, Durbanville, built in 1860

dated 1850, the building has been much altered. Over the years it has been a magistrates' court, a school and a town hall.

Return along Wellington Road and across Main Road; the road continues as Vrede Street. Turn right into Hoog Street and further on the right is **Onze Molen** ⓬, a housing complex clustered around an old mill built circa 1840. The mill has recently been restored and is a reminder that much of this area was farmland before it was changed into housing estates.

Return to Main Road and turn right towards Cape Town. On the left are Baxter Street and **All Saints Church** ⓭. Built as a school chapel to designs by Sophy Gray, the church opened around 1860. Since then it has been extended a few times.

Drive back to Durbanville Avenue (Main Road) and turn left. On the way to the N1 you will see the **Durbanville Rose Garden** ⓮ on the right; its thousands of roses are best seen in late spring or early summer.

The Onze Molen windmill originates from around 1840.

The Kristo Pienaar Environmental Education Centre

Tygerberg Nature Reserve

The Tygerberg Nature Reserve is situated in the northern suburbs of Cape Town near Plattekloof, and is easily accessible from the N1 towards Paarl.

There are different versions as to how the name Tygerberg originated. In 1655 Jan van Riebeeck referred to the area in his diary as the Luipaerts Berghen (Leopard's Mountain) – presumably because, from a distance, the indigenous bushes with their different shades of colour resembled the skin of a leopard. Another view is that when the name was changed to Tijgerberghen in 1661, the settlers used the early Middle Dutch word 'tijger', a name that described both the tiger and the leopard.

A VOC cattle post was established here, and in 1690 Simon van der Stel gave land grants in the area. Also in 1690, a signal

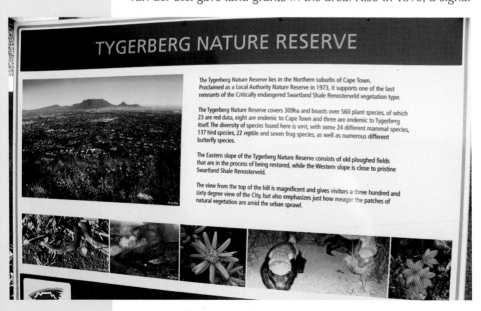

TYGERBERG NATURE RESERVE

The Tygerberg Nature Reserve lies in the Northern suburbs of Cape Town. Proclaimed as a Local Authority Nature Reserve in 1973, it supports one of the last remnants of the Critically endangered Swartland Shale Renosterveld vegetation type.

The Tygerberg Nature Reserve covers 309ha and boasts over 560 plant species, of which 23 are red data, eight are endemic to Cape Town and three are endemic to Tygerberg itself. The diversity of species found here is vast, with some 24 different mammal species, 137 bird species, 22 reptile and seven frog species, as well as numerous different butterfly species.

The Eastern slope of the Tygerberg Nature Reserve consists of old ploughed fields that are in the process of being restored, while the Western slope is close to pristine Swartland Shale Renosterveld.

The view from the top of the hill is magnificent and gives visitors a three hundred and sixty degree view of the City, but also emphasizes just how meager the patches of natural vegetation are amid the urban sprawl.

cannon was placed on the hill with the aim of sending messages to the farmers in the area.

The 309-hectare Tygerberg Nature Reserve was opened by the Bellville Municipality in 1973, and the Kristo Pienaar Environmental Education Centre was established in 1991. The reserve has an aromatic indigenous garden and displays of some of the animals in the sanctuary, which include steenbok, bontebok, caracal, porcupine and mongoose.

The nature reserve protects 560 plant species and 24 mammal species, and 137 bird species have been recorded there. It also preserves a small remnant of renosterveld, a critically endangered vegetation type.

For visitors there are a number of different paths and trails, including a path suitable for wheelchairs. There are also two picnic areas.

The nature reserve is supported by a very active Friends of Tygerberg Hills Group, which arranges hikes and monthly talks.

Two of the reserve's inhabitants: the leopard tortoise and the bontebok

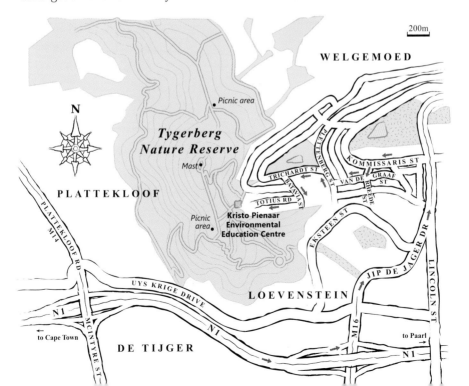

USEFUL INFORMATION

Die Oog Bird Sanctuary
donations box
021 712 1314
www.dieoog.org.za

Intaka Island
admission charge
021 552 6889
www.intaka.co.za

Sanlam Art Gallery
open daily
021 947 3359
www.sanlam.co.za

Van Oudtshoorn's vault
Monte Rosa Old-Age Home
for access
021 423 8173

Best-Kept Secrets

NEWLANDS SPRING

From the early eighteenth century, beer was brewed in Newlands because of the quality of the underground spring water occurring there. In 1859 the Mariendahl Brewery, at the site of the current South African Breweries facility, piped water from this spring. At the end of the cul-de-sac, the overflow water from the spring runs into a channel. People come daily to collect this pure water in containers because they believe it has medicinal qualities. To avoid congestion in the road and inconvenience to residents, South African Breweries have provided a tap, connected via a pipeline to the spring, at the entrance to the brewery in Letterstedt Road, from where the public can fetch water.

Directions: Coming from Claremont, take the Main Road towards Newlands. When you reach the traffic lights opposite the Newlands swimming pool, turn right into Letterstedt Road. The entrance is on the left-hand side. The spring itself is in Springs Way, off Kildare Road, off Newlands Avenue.

Reverend Helperus Ritzema van Lier's grave, Newlands

VAN LIER'S GRAVE – NEWLANDS

Reverend Helperus Ritzema van Lier was a much-respected minister of the Groote Kerk in Cape Town and requested that he be buried in the countryside; he died in 1793. His small burial vault lies in the middle of what was once an unspoiled landscape. Today suburbia has overtaken the countryside!

Location: Van Lier's grave is on the corner of Finsbury and Ravensberg avenues, off Newlands Avenue.

Boshof Gates, Newlands

BOSHOF GATES – NEWLANDS

Passed by thousands of cars daily, these attractive gates in Boshof Avenue mark the entrance to a large farm that dates from 1666. The gates were erected by Alexander van Breda around 1790. The farm was later subdivided and today it is a popular residential area. An old farmhouse remains in Boshof Avenue.

Directions: Parking is not allowed in Paradise Road. To visit the gates, coming from Cape Town on the M3, take the Fernwood Avenue turn-off to the right at the traffic lights and then turn right into Boshof Avenue. When you come from Wynberg on the M3, Fernwood Avenue is on the left.

LIESBEEK RIVER PROJECT – BISHOPSCOURT VILLAGE

A neighbourhood project along the oldest urban river in the Cape has transformed an overgrown riverbank into an idyllic area. The project has concentrated on rehabilitation and conservation of the Liesbeek riverbank.

A seating area, which contains a memorial sundial, is situated along Noreen Avenue. From here a stepped pathway leads down to the river. Local residents fund and maintain this project in conjunction with the City of Cape Town.

Directions: Approaching from Cape Town along the M3, turn right at the traffic lights into Bishopscourt Drive. From here, turn right into Robinson Avenue and right again into Noreen Avenue.

A delightful garden on the banks of the Liesbeek River

VAN OUDTSHOORN'S VAULT – GARDENS

Near the Mount Nelson Hotel, in Faure Street, off Kloof Street, is the only remnant of the demolished Saasveld House designed by Louis Thibault in 1791. The vault, also designed by Thibault, has been restored and is the only reminder of the estates that existed in the area in the late 1700s. The vault was built for Baron William Ferdinand van Rheede van Oudtshoorn. There is a story that the baron insisted that, when he was placed in the tomb, pen and paper should be provided so that he could communicate from the other side!

Directions: Going up Kloof Street towards the mountain, turn left into Wilkinson Street and left into Faure Street (one way). On the right, before the Monte Rosa Old-Age Home, is a gateway. Ring the bell at the back gate of the Home to gain admission. The vault is on the right as you enter the property.

Baron William Ferdinand van Rheede van Oudtshoorn's vault, Gardens

WOTERSEN'S VAULT – GREEN POINT

Pieter Wotersen was one of six purchasers who took ownership of six large estates between the present-day Somerset and High Level roads. Wotersen purchased his estate in 1815. He died in 1827 and his wife had a tomb erected for him on the slopes of Signal Hill. The vault is thought to be the work of Herman Schutte. It is visible from Table Bay and is often used as a visual aid to the navigators of ships entering the Alfred Basin. Wessels Road, in Green Point, is named after a relative of the Wotersen family.

Location: The vault is at the top end of Wessels Road, off Main Road in Green Point.

Pieter Wotersen's vault, Green Point

Grey heron are regularly sighted at Glencairn Vlei.

GLENCAIRN VLEI CONSERVATION AREA

This wetland situated on the Else River in Glencairn has a winding walkway. It is home to a rich variety of bird life and small mammals. There is parking and access to the conservation area in Glen Road, opposite Caithness Road. This area should appeal to the agile, as the paths are narrow and rough in parts. Access can be gained to the beach and tidal pool by an underpass. It is best to go with a companion, as it is fairly isolated. The former Glencairn Hotel, designed by John Parker in 1904, is nearby.

Directions: From the Glencairn Expressway (M6), turn right onto Main Road and then right into Glen Road.

DIE OOG BIRD SANCTUARY – BERGVLIET

Tucked away in a residential suburb is this interesting reminder of a past era. The dam was part of a French-style pleasure garden that belonged to Bergvliet Farm, one of the oldest in the Constantia Valley. A Friends Group has enthusiastically promoted this attractive spot, which has a large variety of bird life.

Directions: Turn off the M3 from Cape Town onto Ladies Mile Road, then right into Homestead Avenue and left into Starke Road. From here, veer right into Mutual Way, left into Lake View Road and right into Midwood Avenue. The entrance is on the right in Midwood Avenue.

Die Oog Bird Sanctuary is a tranquil retreat in the heart of Bergvliet.

SANLAM ART GALLERY – BELLVILLE

One of the largest corporate art collections in South Africa is owned by the financial services company Sanlam. The Sanlam Art Gallery features the works of well-known and emerging South African artists. The gallery is open during office hours.

Location: The Sanlam Art Gallery is on the ground floor of the Sanlam Head Office, Voortrekker Road, Bellville.

INTAKA ISLAND – CENTURY CITY

In the middle of the large Century City mixed-use development is a 16-hectare multi-purpose nature area. It is home to 212 types of indigenous plants and 120 bird species, including a number of waterbirds. Started in 1996, it has an eco centre, nature walks and bird hides. It is open daily and boat rides are available.

Directions: Intaka Island is well signposted from Bosmansdam Road and the N1 entrances to Century City on the way to Bellville.

Intaka Island

Bibliography

Athiros, G. and L. (editors). *Woodstock: A Selection of Articles from the Woodstock Whisperer 2003–2007.* Cape Town: Historical Media. 2007.

Botha, G.C. *Place Names in the Cape Province.* Cape Town: Juta. 1926.

Cape Mazaar (Kramat) Society. *Guide to the Kramats of the Western Cape.* 2001.

Cape Times Peninsula Directory 1962/3. Cape Times. 1962.

Cape Trams: From Horse to Diesel. Cape Town: Fraser Gill and Associates. 1961.

Cobern, J. *Fish Hoek Looking Back.* Fish Hoek Printing and Publishing. 2003.

Crump, A. and Van Niekerk, R. *Public Sculpture and Reliefs.* Cape Town: Clifton Publications. 1988.

Dane, P. and Wallace, S-A. *The Great Houses of Constantia.* Cape Town: Don Nelson. 1981

Davenport, R. and Saunders, C. *South Africa: A Modern History.* London: Macmillan Press. 2000.

De Villiers, S. *A Tale of Three Cities.* Cape Town: Murray & Roberts. 1985.

Fransen, H. *The Old Buildings of the Cape.* Cape Town: Jonathan Ball Publishers. 2004.

Hart, P. *Rondebosch and Rosebank Street Names.* Cape Town: Peter Hart. 1998.

Hart, P. *A Bowlful of Names.* Cape Town: The Historical Society of Cape Town. 2011.

Harris, C.J. and Ingpen, B. *Mailships of the Union-Castle Line.* Cape Town: Fernwood Press. 1994.

Law, B. *Papenboom in Newlands: Cradle of the Brewing Industry.* Cape Town: Beatrice Law. 2007.

Manuel, G. *I Remember Cape Town.* Cape Town: Don Nelson Publishers. 1997.

Manuel, G. and Hatfield, D. *District Six.* Cape Town: Penguin Southern Africa. 1976.

Martin, D. *The Bishop's Churches.* Cape Town: Struik Publishers. 2005.

Martin, D. *Walking Long Street.* Cape Town: Struik Publishers. 2007.

Mountain, A. *An Unsung Heritage: Perspectives on Slavery.* Cape Town: David Philip Publishers. 2004.

Muir, J. *Know Your Cape.* Cape Town: Howard Timmins. 1975.

Muir, J. *Guide to Cape Town and the Western Cape.* Cape Town: Howard Timmins. 1976.

Oberholster, J.J. *The Historical Monuments of South Africa.* Stellenbosch: The Rembrandt van Rijn Foundation for Culture. 1972.

Picton-Seymour, D. *Victorian Buildings in South Africa.* Cape Town: A.A. Balkema. 1977.

Picton-Seymour, D. *Historical Buildings in South Africa.* Cape Town: Struikhof Publishers. 1989.

Rennie, J. (editor). *The Buildings of Central Cape Town.* Cape Town: Cape Provincial Institute of Architects. 1978.

Richings, G. *The Life and Work of Charles Michell.* Simon's Town: Fernwood Press. 2006.

Robinson, H. *Wynberg: A Special Place.* Wynberg: Houghton House. 2001.

Robinson, H. *Villages of the Liesbeeck: From the Sea to the Source.* Wynberg: Houghton House. 2011.

Rosenthal, E. (editor). *Encyclopedia of Southern Africa* (6th edition). London: Frederick Warne and Co. Ltd. 1973.

Ryan, R. *A City that Changed it's Face.* Cape Town: McKerrow Atkins Publishers. 1981.

Schrire, G. in association with Hillel Turok. *Camps Bay: An Illustrated History.* Lakeside: A.W. Louw. 2003.

Shaw, G. *Believe in Miracles.* Cape Town: Ampersand Press. 2007.

Shorten, J.R. *Cape Town: The Golden Jubilee of Cape Town.* Cape Town: John R. Shorten Pty. Ltd. 1963.

Simon's Town Historical Society. *Our Simon's Town.* 1999.

Sisson, T. *Just Nuisance A.B.* Cape Town: W.J. Flesch and Partners Pty Ltd. 1985.

Townsend, L. and Townsend, S. *Bokaap Faces and Facades.* Cape Town: Howard Timmins. 1977.

Tredgold, A. *The Ardernes and their Garden: A Family Chronicle.* Cape Town: Arderne Book Trust. 1990.

Van der Ross, R.E. *Up from Slavery: Slaves at the Cape.* Cape Town: Ampersand Press. 2005.

Van der Ross, R.E. *Buy my Flowers!: The story of Strawberry Lane, Constantia.* Cape Town: Ampersand Press. 2007.

Wagener, F.J. (editor). *Rondebosch Down the Years: 1657 to 1957.*

Walker, M. *Muizenberg: A Forgotten Place.* St James: Michael Walker. 2009.

Walker, M. *Kalk Bay: A Place of Character.* St James: Michael Walker. 2010.

Weston, J. *Outcast Cape Town.* Cape Town: Human and Rousseau. 1981.

Worden, N., Van Heyningen, E. and Bickford-Smith, V. *Cape Town, The Making of a City: An Illustrated Social History.* Cape Town: David Philip Publishers. 1999.

Index

Page numbers in *italics*
refer to pictures.

34 Plein Street 56
71 Roeland Street 56
175 Long Street *42,*

A
Adderley Street 32–35
Admiralty House *94,* 94
Aerial Ropeway 96
African Station Club 97
Al-Azhar Mosque *154,* 156
Albertyn's Cottage 100
Albion Spring *131,* 131–132
Alfred Basin *66,* 69
Aljam Mosque *60,* 61
All Saints Church,
    Durbanville *182,* 183
Alphen Hotel *172,* 172
Altydgedaght wine estate
    181
Anglo-Boer War
    memorials 51, *101*
apartheid *98,* 98, 155, 177
    See also forced removals;
    Group Areas Act
Arderne Gardens *129,* 129
Argus Building 37
Atlas sculpture *37,* 37
Atlas Trading Company 61
Atwell Baking Company
    98, 98
Auwal Mosque 58
Avenue House 139

B
Bailey's Cottage 111
Bailey, Sir Abe, grave 114
Baker, Sir Herbert 163
Balmoral Hotel 119
Barnard, Lady Anne *50,*
    127
Barnard, Professor
    Christiaan 136
bathing boxes,
    Muizenberg *110*
Beaufort Cottage 106
Belvedere 164
Belvedere Hotel 56
Bertram House Museum 21
Blaauwberg Conservation
    Area 180
Blouberg and Durbanville
    178–183
Blouberg Hill, Battle 161,
    181
Blue Lodge *44,* 44
Bo-Kaap *57,* 57–61, *61*
Bo-Kaap Museum *58,* 58
bontebok *185*
Boom, Hendrik 14
Boshof Gates, Newlands
    186

Botha, Louis *56,* 56
Boulders Beach 150, *151*
Boyes Drive 109
Braeside 113
breakwater *67,* 67
Britannia, statue *34*
British Hotel *97,* 97
broekie lace *42,* 43
Bromwell Hotel *160,* 160
Buffelsfontein Visitors
    Centre 149–150
Buitenverwachting *169,* *170*

C
Cableway, Table Mountain
    11
Caledon Street Police
    Station 55
Camel Rock 149
Camps Bay 88–91
Canty Bay House *114,*
    114–115
Cape Flats 176–177
Cape Medical Museum 83
Cape Minstrel Carnival
    59, 59
Cape of Good Hope Nature
    Reserve 149–150
Cape Quarter Lifestyle
    Centre 78
Cape Technical College
    54–55
Cape Tourist Guides
    Association 176
Cape Town City Council
    crest *118*
Cape Town City Hall *51,* 51
Cape Town Holocaust
    Centre 18
Cape Town Stadium 82
Cape Town Tourism 176
Carrisbrooke 113
Casa Labia *115,* 115
Castle Brewery 161
Castle of Good Hope
    51–52, *52,* 53
Cellars-Hohenhort hotel,
    The 172
Central Hotel 98
Central Methodist Mission
    Church *28,* 28
Centre for the Book 22
Ceolnaraba 113
Chapel Street Primary
    School 157
Chapman's Peak Drive
    145, 148–149, *149*
Chavonnes Battery 70
C.H. Pearne & Company
    32, 33
Christmas bands 59
Church of St Francis 94
Church of St Simon and
    St Jude *101,* 101

Church of the Good
    Shepherd, plaque *152,*
    152
Church Square 26
Church Street Antiques
    Market 27
Circle of Islam 61
City and Civil Service Club
    22, 22
City Hall *51,* 51
Claremont 126–129
clock towers 70, *71, 116*
Colosseum Cinema 36–37
Company's Garden 14–19
Congregational Church,
    Claremont *128,* 128
Constantia and Tokai
    167–173
Constantia Cemetery 172,
    173, 173
Coolarty 113
Coornhoop 134
crafts, Philippi, Cape Flats
    176, 177
Criterion Cinema 99
Cut, the *69,* 69

D
Dalebrook tidal pool 105
Danger Beach 105
de Almeida, Dom
    Francisco 158
De Beers Building 97
de la Quellerie, Maria 35
Delville Wood Memorial
    17, 17
Devil's Peak 12
De Waal Park and
    Gardens *62,* 62–65, *63*
De Waterkant *76,* 78
Dias, Bartholomew 35, 150
Die Oog Bird Sanctuary,
    Bergvliet 188
District Six 154–157
District Six Museum *54,*
    54, *154*
dog drinking fountain 86
Dorp Street Mosque *45,* 45
Drie Koppen 138
Drill Hall 51
Duncan Dock 72
Durbanville and Blouberg
    178–183
Durbanville Rose Garden
    183
Dutch Reformed Church,
    100, 101, *124,* 124, *181,*
    181

E
East City 48–56
East Fort 148
Edwardian villas 118
Edward VII, King 51

Egyptian Building *20,* 20
Equity House 37

F
Fan Walk 76–78
Ferryman's Tavern 74
fire station, in harbour 72
First National Bank
    Building 34
fishermen's cottages, Kalk
    Bay *108,* 109
Fish Hoek 103
flower market *32,* 34
forced removals *54,* *98,*
    98, 109, 152, 155, 157,
    169, *171,* 171, 177
    See also apartheid;
    Group Areas Act
Foreshore 36
Fort Wynyard 82
free burghers 131, 135
French Redoubt 159

G
Gardens Centre 63
Gardens and De Waal
    Park 62–65
Gardens Presbyterian
    Church 65
Genadendal 133
Geological Exposure *87,* 87
German Settlers, Philippi
    177, 177
Glebe Cottage 124
Glencairn Vlei
    Conservation Area 188
Glendower Hotel 140
Golden Acre Centre 35
Gold of Africa Museum *30,*
    30–31
Government Avenue *10,* *14*
Graaff's Pool 87
Graceland 113
Grand Central Post Office
    50
Grand Daddy Hotel *47,* 47
Grand Drive 146–153
Grand Parade 50–51
Gray, Bishop Robert 39
Great Synagogue 18
Greenmarket Square *24,*
    27–29
Green Point 79–83
Green Point Common
    79–82
Green Point Lighthouse
    80, 80–81
Green Point Memorial
    Wall *82,* 82–83
Green Point Urban Park
    79, 80, *81,* 81
Grey, Sir George 16
Groeneveld (Green Fields)
    131

Groot Constantia 151, 167, *171*, 171–172
Groote Kerk 26, 42
Groote Schuur Manor House 133
Group Areas Act of 1950 155
See also apartheid; forced removals
Gunners' Memorial 17

H
Harbour Café 69
harbour development 36
Harbour Mansions 108
Heart of Cape Town Museum 136
Heerengracht 35–36
Herbert Baker buildings 118, *119*
Heritage Museum 100
Heritage Square 29–30
Herschel Obelisk 127
Hiddingh Campus 20–22
Hiddingh Hall 20–21
Highfield Road 139
hippos *174*, 174–175
Hofmeyr family vault 65
Hofmeyr, Jan Hendrik 27, 27
Holy Cross Centre, District Six 157
Holy Trinity Church *106*, 106, *107*
Hospital Terrace 101
Houses of Parliament *9*, 19
Hout Bay 147–148
Hurling Pump 63–64

I
Imhoff Farm 149
inclined railway 101
Intaka Island, Century City *188*, 188
Irma Stern Museum 140
Iziko Bertram House Museum 21
Iziko Bo-Kaap Museum *58*, 58
Iziko Maritime Centre 74
Iziko Planetarium 17
Iziko Rust en Vreugd Museum 55–56
Iziko Slave Lodge 24–25, *25*
Iziko South African Museum 17
Iziko South African National Gallery 18

J
Jacobs Ladder 105
Jager's Walk *102*, 102–103
Jamia Mosque *60*, 61
Jansen Hall 180
Japanese lantern 15–16

Japonica Walk *164*, 164
Jewish Museum 18
Jonkershuis Restaurant 172
Josephine Mill *132*, 132
Jubilee Square 98–99
Just Nuisance *95* , 95, *99*

K
Kalk Bay *104*, 104–109
Kilindini 140
Kimberley Hotel 56
Kingsley, Mary 94
Kirstenbosch National Botanical Garden 152
Klein Constantia wine estate *166*, 169
Knight's Villa *114*, 114
Koopmans de Wet House 31
Kristo Pienaar Environmental Education Centre *184*, 185
Krotoa Place *36*, 37

L
Lady of Hope 82, *83*
Langley Cottage 122
Lankester Building 96
La Plaisance 120
Leonard Gill Museum 175
leopard sculpture *148*, 148
leopard tortoise *185*
Liesbeek River Project, Bishopscourt Village *187*, 187
Liesbeek River Trail *130*, 130–133
Liesbeek River Walk *134*, 134–136
Lightfoot, Archdeacon Thomas Fothergill 50
lion gateway 17
Lion's Head 13
Lister Arboretum 169
Little Chelsea *120*, 120
Little Theatre *20*, 20
Litvins Private Kosher Hotel 118
Long Cottage 113
Long Street 40–47
Long Street Baths 44
Lord Nelson Hotel 96
Lukin, Major General Sir Henry 16
Lutheran Church complex 30, *31*
Lutheran Church, Philippi *176*, 177

M
magistrates' court 55
Magnolia Cottage 122
Mahmud, Sayed *169*, 169
Majestic Mansions 118
Mandela Rhodes Building *37*, 38

manganese mine jetty *148*, 148
Mariendahl Brewery *132*, 186
Maritime Centre 74
Market House *29*, 29
Martello Tower 101
Maynardville Open-Air Theatre 125
Mead, Pinelands *141*, 142
Melkbosstrand 180
memorial urns, University of Cape Town 165
Methodist Chapel 97, 144
Methodist Church 120, *140*, 140
Metropolitan Golf Course 81
Michaelis School of Fine Art 21
milestones 113, 133
Millionaires' Row 113–115
Millstone Farm Stall and Café *141*, 144
Milton Pool 87
Mission Church, Wynberg 125
Model Villa 63
Molteno Power Station and Reservoir 65
money tree 108
Montebello Design Centre 129
Moravian Chapel, District Six *157*, 157
Mostert's Mill 139
Mouille Point Lighthouse See Green Point Lighthouse
Mountain Club of South Africa 11
Mount Nelson Hotel *65*, 65
Mowbray 137–140
Mowbray Hotel 138
Mowbray Town Hall *138*, 138
Muizenberg and St James 110–116
Muizenberg, Battle 114
Muizenberg railway station 115
Muizenberg Village 117–119
Muller's Optometrists 48
Murray, Rev. Andrew 32, *33*
Mutual Heights *48*, 48

N
National Library of South Africa 16, 22
New Apostolic Church, District Six 157
Newlands Spring 186
Nieuw Haarlem, shipwreck 180
Nobel Square *74*, 74
Noon Gun *13*, 13

Noorul Mosque 100
Nuisance, Just *95*, 95, *99*

O
Observatory See South African Astronomical Observatory
Odd Fellows Hall 120
Old Biscuit Mill *158*, 160, *161*
old Granary Building *8*, 52
Oldham's Field 118
old Medical School *20*, 21, 21
Old Mutual Building *48*, 48
old shoreline 70
Old Thatch Cottage 126
Old Town House 28
Olympia Picture House 108
Ons Huisie 180
Onze Molen *183*, 183
Oranjezicht 62–63
outspans 108,132

P
padraos 150, 150
Palace Barracks 94
Palm Tree Mosque 42, *43*
Pan African Market *45*, 45
Parade 50–51
Parliament 19
Pass-Law protests: The 1960 March 55
peace stone 34
pelicans *175*
penguins 150, *151*, 180
Penny Ferry 69
Penrose 139
Perseverance Tavern 55
Philly, the horse *90*, 90
Phoenix House 100
Pinelands 141–144
port captain's office *68*, 69
Portswood Ridge 69, 74
Posthuys 115
Prestwich Memorial *78*, 78
Prince Alfred Hotel 96
Princess Vlei *175*, 175
Proteas, Kirstenbosch National Botanical Garden 152
Protea Village 152
pump house, in harbour 73

Q
Queen Victoria, statue *7*, 19
Queen Victoria Street 22–23

R
Race Classification Appeal Board 22
Red Lion Hotel 56
Rhodes, Cecil John *16*, 113–114, 152–153, *153*, 164, *165*

Rhodes Recreational
Ground *137*, 140
Rietvlei 180
Rio Grande Hotel 118
Ritchie Building 22
RMS *Athens*, shipwreck 83
Robben Island *72*, 72
Robinson Graving Dock 73
Rocket Life-saving
Apparatus Store 74
Roman Catholic Church,
District Six 157
Roman Rock Lighthouse
150
Rondebosch 162–165
Rondebosch Common
165, 165
Rondebosch Fountain *133*,
133, 164
Rondebosch Library *130*
Rondebosch Town Hall
130
Rondevlei Nature Reserve
174, 174–175
Rosebank Place *64*, 64
Rosebank Station 134
Rosedale 22
Rose Street *58*
Rotunda, The *91*, 91
Roundhouse, The 91
Runciman's Building 97
Rustenberg Junior School
for Girls 164
Rust en Vrede Cultural
Centre, Durbanville
181, 183
Rust en Vrede,
Muizenberg 114
Ruth Prowse School of Art
160, 160

S

Sanlam Art Gallery 188
Sartorial House 99
Savoy Cinema 140
Schweppes emblem *131*
Scott, Robert Falcon 36
Scotts Building 50
Seafarer rescue 86, 87
Seaforth Burying Ground
101
Sea Point 35, 84–87
sea walkway, Muizenberg
to Kalk Bay 110–111, *111*
Signal Hill 13, 147
Silvermine 151
Simon's Town 92–101
Sir Abe Bailey's grave 114
Skaife's Barn *150*, 150
Slave Church Museum
46, 47
Slave Lodge 24–25, *25*
slavery 26, *27*, 27
slave tree 26
Smuts, Jan, statues *18*,
18–19, *24*, 24

South African Air Force
Museum 179
South African
Astronomical
Observatory 136
South African National
Gallery 18
South African Naval
Museum *96*, 96
South African Slave
Church Museum *46*, 47
South African Turf Club 81
Southern Floe, shipwreck
memorial 142
Southern Right Whale *103*
Spracklen, W.J. &
Company 56
Springfield Convent school
124
squirrels *15*
Standard Bank Building
34
St Andrew's Presbyterian
Church 78
St Andrew's Square 78
Star of the Sea Convent
112
Steenberg main house
168, 168
Steenberg Vineyards 168
St Francis Anglican
Church 94
St George's buildings 99
St George's Cathedral
22, *23*
St George's Mall 36–39
St James and Muizenberg
110–116
St James Catholic Church
112, 112
St James post office
112–113
St James Retirement
Centre 111–112
St John the Evangelist
Anglican Church 124
St Mark's Anglican Church
156, 156
St Martini German
Lutheran Church 44
St Mary's Cathedral 56
St Michael's Catholic
Church 130
stone church, Porter
Reformatory *169*, 169
stonework, in Kalk Bay
106
St Paul's Anglican Church
133
St Philip's Anglican
Church 157
St Philip's Mission Chapel
157
Strawberry Lane 169,
171, 171
St Saviour's Church 128

St Simon and St Jude
Catholic Church *101*, 101
St Stephen's Anglican
Chapel 142, *143*
St Stephen's Church 29,
30, 30
Studland 94
Stuttafords department
store 34
Summer House 164
Sunny Cove Station 103

T

Table Mountain *10*, 11,
10–12, *12*, *63*, *66*, *179*
Table Mountain Aerial
Cableway 11
Tafelberg Dutch Reformed
Church 55
Tana Baru Cemetery 60
Tenterden 123
Theatre on the Bay 90
The Criterion 99
The Majestic appartment
complex 106–107
The Palms 161
Tidal Pool, Sea Point 87
time-ball tower 74, *75*
Tokai and Constantia
167–173
Tokai Forest 169
Tokai Manor House 169
toll gate 159
Treaty Tree 160–161, *161*
Trojan Horse memorial
177
Trovato House *163*, 163
Tuynhuys *19*, 19
Twelve Apostles 147
Two Oceans Aquarium
73, 73
Tygerberg Nature Reserve
184, 184–185, *185*

U

Union-Castle Line 74,
75, *50*
Unitarian Church 47
United Services Institute
97, 97
University of Cape Town
162
Ustings, Catharina 168

V

Valkenberg Manor House
134
Van der Stel, Simon 15, 17,
112, 151, 171–172
Van Hunks, legend 12
Van Lier's Grave,
Newlands *186*, 186
Van Oudtshoorn's vault,
Gardens *187*, 187
Van Riebeeck, Jan 14, 26,
35, 120

V&A Waterfront 66–75
Victoria and Alfred Hotel
65
Victoria Basin 72
Victoria Drive, Oudekraal
146
Victorian houses,
Mowbray *139*
Victoria Road, Camps Bay
88, 89
Villa Capri 105
Village Square, Wynberg
123
Vineyard Hotel *126*, 127
Volunteer Drill Hall 51
Von Dessin, J.N. 22

W

Waggenaar's dam 35
Warrior Toy Museum 100
Waterfront 66–75
Welgelegen Farm gates
139
Wellington Fruit Growers
Building 50
Westerford Arms Hotel
133
Westgate Terrace 97
whalers' cottages,
Muizenberg *116*, 118
whaling 109
white horses, as *Seafarer*
rescue memorial 87
Whytes Building 98
Widow Twankey *39*, 39
Willetts Masonic Hotel 98
Winchester Mansions
Hotel *85*, 86
Wolmunster 139
Woltemade, Wolraad 144
wooden bridge, Milnerton
178, 179
Woodstock 158–161
Woolsack 164
World War 1 memorial,
Observatory *136*, 136
Wotersen's vault, Green
Point *187*, 187
Wynberg 120–125
Dutch Reformed Church
124, 124
Mission Church 125
Town Hall *122*, 122
Village Square 123
Wynberg Park 125
Wynyard Battery 82

Y

Yokohama 114

Z

Zeenatul Islam Mosque
157
Zonnebloem College 157